YOU...GOD
Connecting the Dots

A guidebook for discovering your path
to true empowerment

By Dana Winter

Published 2019
ISBN: 978-0-578-52590-7

Harmony-Publishing
7963 Royal Arms Court
St. Louis, MO 63123

DEDICATION AND
SPECIAL NOTE TO READER

This book is dedicated to anyone who is desiring to look deeper into their own story and discover the existence of a creative, loving presence that has always been interacting with them. In this book, I primarily refer to that presence as God but also use such descriptors as Light, Love, Higher Self, Authentic Self, Creative Energy and All That Is. The key is not to get bogged down with a name but instead become aware that you have been engaging with and interacting with this loving creative energy all along. Please feel free to replace the name God with any name or names that resonate with you.

ACKNOWLEDGEMENTS

Special thanks to my editor, Vincent Rhomberg, who got this book off my computer and into your hands. Also, special thanks to Maria Verbeck for all of her support and the cover art. Thank you to all of my students who shared in the development of this material. And thank you to Mary Feagan for allowing me to use her poem "Old Judge God" in this book.

TABLE OF CONTENTS

Preface
The Authentic Life

I remember, about 25 years ago, becoming so enamored with the word "authentic." It simply fascinated me. I found myself thinking, "What would it be like to be nothing but real, nothing but true to myself?" I recall reading stories about people feeling as if they were a fake in their own lives and thinking it was just a matter of time before others called them on their game. Many of them chose to walk away from their "successful" lives to pursue something that felt more real, more true. In my own life, I felt as if I had created such a great façade that even I didn't know who was hidden beneath it.

So, one day, I decided that I wanted to be authentic. I declared it for myself. I closed my eyes and imagined myself pulling off huge layers of "shoulds, shouldn'ts and can'ts" and tossing them over some imaginary ledge in my mind. I watched them getting smaller and smaller until they disappeared from my mind's eye. I knew that being honest with myself and others would be a challenge to my people-pleasing personality, but I thought I was ready.

What I didn't realize at the time was that everything that was not true to who I am, would need to be cleared away. What I didn't realize was that there was a presence listening, a presence who had read what was written on my mind and heart. And that this presence had the incredible ability to take my thoughts and feelings and turn them into a reality. Later it all made sense, but at the time it seemed as if my old life was suddenly being taken away from me. I felt as if my decision to be true to myself was hurting people that I cared about, and that the "shoulds, shouldn'ts and can'ts" were making a big comeback. I felt that the guilt and depression were more than I could handle. It made me want to run back to my old life, but when I considered that possibility, I found myself sapped of all energy. I felt as if my old life was no longer an option; it had been taken off the table. My body let me know that Dana doesn't live there anymore.

In retrospect, I realize that my essential self not only knew what I desired, but it held the blueprint for my authentic life. Once I had made the choice to move forward with that life, the first order of business was to dismantle the façade; my artificial self would have to go. Bulldozers arrived in the form of people passionate about their lives, their work and their relationships. They provided a sharp contrast to the lack of passion I felt for my existing life. I didn't know where I was going, but I knew that where I had been was no longer livable.

Living in between the "old" and the "yet to come" was scary, but it led me to journaling, to reaching out and asking if anyone was there who could hear me and help me out of my confusion and pain. I remember sitting in the silence, my pen resting on the blank page, hoping for an answer. After a few moments, a comforting voice began giving me one word at a time. I was simply taking dictation not knowing what the author would say next but feeling the tension in my body beginning to ease. I was told that it was all going to be alright, that I was doing really well and that my life was unfolding perfectly. I was told that the lives of the others involved were also on purpose, that there was mutual growth going on here, and that just beneath the pain felt by the personality was joy. I doubted that this was true, but the internal voice continued to soothe me. I returned often to the page and still do. There is a comforter within us, a knower, a builder, a coordinator. This one holds the blueprint of the truth of who we are, and for that one nothing is impossible.

My personality has been through this process several times, and I now see it as God, the dynamic, creative energy, expressing as my authentic self, doing Its work. I now see that it is going on all the time in all of our lives. I now realize that we all go through many phases of the demolition of our artificial selves followed by new construction and expansion, and that it is all good and we are all doing really well. I share this with you in case you feel as if everything is falling apart, and you don't know what can possibly be built in its place, or how you will find the resources to build it. There is one within you that knows and handles all of the details. I am now living my best life, and I know that there is much more good to come. I now know and trust that we all have within us the most incredible architect just waiting for us to say yes to our authentic life.

Much love, peace and joy,
Dana

―――――――――――

"What we are looking for is
what is looking."
— St. Francis of Assisi
1181 – 1226

―――――――――――

Introduction
Breaking Up Is Hard to Do

In 2010 I created a class called *Connecting the Dots*. The purpose of the class was for the students to find proof of a connection between their thoughts, feelings and beliefs and their actual experiences. The response to the class was so positive that I began writing this book.

I finished the first draft quickly, but the growth of Harmony Fellowship, the New Thought group that I founded in 2008, caused me to set the book aside. In 2012 I returned to it, but with major changes going on in my life, the book was once again moved to the back burner and left to simmer. A couple of years later I returned to the book but found myself questioning my motives for writing it. Did the world really need another book? There are so many spiritual books already available. But then, one evening while teaching the class in 2014, I encountered a student who was very distressed.

She told me that she just could not shake the feeling that she was innately bad. She had the sense that God was always watching her and judging her. I was surprised that the student was experiencing such a fear of God as she had been attending New Thought churches for quite some time, and I thought she had accepted the central belief that we are one with God, a pure creative loving energy.

If you are not familiar with the term New Thought, it refers to a movement that originated in the 19th-century. Its fundamental teaching is that spirit is more real and more powerful than matter, and that the mind has the power to heal our body, our lives and our world. Major

1

groups within this movement include Divine Science, Unity and the Church of Religious Science.

Most New Thought religions are based on Christianity and view Jesus as a great metaphysical teacher. They feel his "miracles" serve to reveal that we all are one with God, a pure loving creative energy, that is always expressing and creating through our thoughts, feelings and beliefs. But, in reality, these teachings are not about a Christian God. They are not about religion at all. Instead, they are about a creative energy that has always been working through us and as us. Jesus is just one example of a person who, through living his own life authentically, discovered a very personal non-religious God within himself. He then began to consciously work with this creative energy.

"Believe me when I say that I am in the Father and the Father is in me;
or at least believe on the evidence of the works themselves."
— John 14:11

Pausing the class, I began talking to the student and she shared that she had recently lost her mother, a God-fearing woman who worried constantly. The God this student feared, the one she had been taught about by her mother and others, was still causing her distress. I suggested that her relationship with God was unhealthy and that she completely break up with *that* God. The class laughed at this suggestion, but in truth, I believe it is what so many of us need to do.

Let's face it, if you had an individual in your life who followed you everywhere, tested you, punished you, required sacrifices and demanded you worship them, you would be running to the nearest courthouse to get a restraining order. You might even consider relocating to a new city and changing your name. But with an ever-present, all-knowing and all-powerful judging God there is no escape. This is the God that many of us learned about as we were growing up. If on some level, you still believe in this "Old Judge God" instead of a pure loving God, then you are in a dysfunctional relationship.

Like all unhealthy relationships, this relationship keeps you off-balance, thrives on drama and is riddled with contradictions. For example, this God who supposedly loves unconditionally and shows compassion, is the same God who required His own son to die for the sins of mankind, the mankind that He created. Does that make any sense to you? Did it ever make sense? Or was this story taught to you by others when you were very young, by the big people, by the ones in the know—a story that also required that you never question it lest you be one of those left behind, one of those doomed to burn in Hell?

Does it make sense that the God who created everything would also create a place called Hell where he could punish his own creations in one of his own creations? Instead of describing a loving God, doesn't this description sound more like a very unhealthy, unstable individual? And yet well-intentioned adults teach these stories to little children and adults alike with the cross or the crucifix serving as a constant reminder of the horrific sacrifice that was required…because of us. It is no wonder that so many of us, like my distressed student, are living in a state of guilt and fear.

But imagine that you could erase from your mind all that you think that you know about God, all that you were taught, and instead let your life teach you about God. You would have to be willing to let go of all your preconceived ideas. You would have to learn to be comfortable living in the emptiness of no story. It is understandable if the idea of dropping the well-established stories fills you with fear. But even that fear shines a light upon your own concept of God. Why would you fear

God? Why would you fear letting go of the stories of a God given to you by others?

If we believe God is everything and a part of everyone, then whatever is true about God would be available to all, even those who have never heard of the religious stories that were given to you; even those who live on a remote island. Use this as your litmus: If it is not available to all, then it is superfluous to God. That is not to say that many enlightened individuals from the stories did not exist but removing them from the pedestals that they've been placed upon will make room for Truth.

The suggestion to walk away from everything you know about God may seem like a dangerous proposition, but if you have, on some level, low self-esteem and a tendency to tolerate unhealthy relationships, I suggest that you look deeper than your own family history for the cause and see if you aren't also living on some level in a relationship with a toxic God. If you think that you've been seeking a close connection with God, but at the same time fear the God you seek, then I can assure you that a big part of you doesn't want to find *that* God. The truth is that you cannot truly love someone you fear. You cannot trust and connect with someone who is threatening your well-being today as well as your "life-ever-after." You cannot have an intimate relationship with someone who gives you freewill and then uses your choices to punish you. So, there is only one thing left for you to do. In order to move forward, to see dramatic changes in your life, you will need to break up with the God of your old understanding, the God of the religious stories. You will need to be open to a new concept of God and a new understanding. You will need to allow yourself to be a student and let God teach you about God.

But how would that happen? What would that look like? Consider that you have been in a classroom with proof of God in your life all along but because of all the stories given to you by others you could not really see God. Imagine that you are now enrolling in a class called, *You…God, Connecting the Dots*, a class where you have chosen to examine your life and see if you can find proof of God woven into the fabric of your own life; not the God you were taught about by others, but a healthy God, a consistently loving God, a God that makes sense to you, a God of your understanding.

————————————

"Truth is not introduced into the individual from without,
but was within, all the time."
— Søren Kierkegaard
May 5, 1813 – November 11, 1855

————————————

Take a look at the questions on the next page. Exploring your introduction to God is a great place to begin.

INTRODUCTORY QUESTIONS

1. Who first introduced you to the concept of God?

2. Was that God loving, friendly, compassionate, judgmental, exclusive or a mixture of those traits?

3. Are you open to the possibility that the judgmental God of religions never existed?

Letting go of everything we've been taught is an important part of our spiritual journey. At some point the words and teachings of others need to be put away so that we can find the voice of a loving presence speaking into our own lives. Without the stories given to us by others we begin to genuinely listen and learn experientially. Allowing everything we think we know about God and ourselves to drop away, we create an opening that allows us to share our deepest feelings and ask all of our questions. The answers are key to remembering who we truly are and why we are here. These honest conversations with God move each of us deeper and deeper into a dynamic personal relationship and ongoing spiritual growth.

————

"We must be ready and willing to perceive new truth even though it is the reverse of what we have believed. We must not let ourselves be bound by what we conceive to be the highest teaching . . . [Such an attitude] warps us and eventuates in spiritual dullness, in stagnation; and stagnation is death. We must keep alive, growing.
That is the Law of Life."
— Nona L. Brooks, a founder of Divine Science
March 22, 1861 – March 14, 1945

—————————

* * * * * * *

That Old Judge God

That Old Judge God is walking away.

He's finished now.

He was as much God as I could imagine at the time.

I used to think that Old Judge God didn't want me to have you.

Now I know he never even existed.

Well, he's walking away now.

I see him shuffling down a dirt road.

He's dragging a ragged black robe behind his bare sagging ass.

I'm ready for Grandmama God now.

I'm ready for big-hearted, big-breasted Grandmama God.

I'm ready for big-hearted, big-handed Granddaddy God.

I'm ready for a God bigger than fourteen skies

bigger than the color orange expanded out beyond all directions

bigger than my longing for fullness multiplied to forty zillion

bigger than my feeling of fullness when I am dancing with you

and everyone we love is clapping stars to us.

Chapter 1
Connecting the Dots

"Joys are our wings; sorrows our spurs."
— *Jean Paul Richter*
June 7, 1847 – August 25, 1937

This is a guidebook for reviewing your past and discovering a very personal and loving God intimately woven into every detail of your life. By laying out significant life events, and seeing them with new eyes, you will discover that there has always been more going on than you realized. What you thought were random events actually fit together forming the shape of you. Each experience has propelled you forward to the next and the next. In the course of connecting the dots between these life events, you will begin to realize that you have always been, and currently are, on a powerful journey, a journey to empowerment. And you have not been traveling alone.

You have always been on this journey, unconsciously following a map imprinted on your heart by your authentic self, your soul, before coming into this physical plane. Discovering this navigational tool will allow you to begin making sense of your life and making peace with everyone and everything in it. *You…God, Connecting the Dots* is about climbing out of the events of your daily life and seeing your experiences from a higher perspective. From this point of view, you can begin to see your life as an evolution and recognize how each individual and every event is an attempt to move you forward to your own truth, your authentic self. You will also see how some of your choices have moved you in the opposite direction, but those choices did not erase your soul's trajectory. Something or someone always came along to guide you back to your path.

If you view these same events strictly from the perspective of your personality—your sense of identity based upon your cumulative physical, mental, emotional and social experiences—then you may interpret these experiences merely as things that "happened to you." This often becomes the basis for the identity of Victim. A victim is one who believes that they have very little control over their lives; that things just happen to them. A victim spends a great part of their time thinking and talking about what "they" did to them. The "they" could be their parents, the political system, their boss, children, boyfriend, or spouse, and even God. Falling into a victim mentality makes you believe that what happened to you is more important than where it is taking you. Believing that things are out of your control and happening to you without reason creates a life filled with fear. Many people live their entire lives caught in this false identity.

If instead, you could see and value what your experiences have taught you, how they have urged you to move forward to a more truthful and authentic life, you would see that everything has always been on purpose. You would also have a glimpse of the personal map that is being navigated by your soul.

This map is easily charted when you begin to recognize the existence of spiritual laws and how they shape your experiences. These spiritual laws, often referred to as the Universal Laws, have been impersonally and consistently running beneath the surface of your life just as the Law of Gravity has been operating in your physical world. We'll look further at the Universal Laws in Chapter 3.

Right now, choose to become an observer of your own life. For just a few minutes connect with your breath. Take a nice deep breath.

Breath in through your nose, deep down into your belly, extending the lower abdomen, and then slowly release the air through slightly pursed lips, until all of the air is released. Do this several times as you continue to read on the next page.

MEDITATION

In this space, I choose to recognize how I got to this present moment, holding this book in my hands and reading these words. I choose to see beyond the physical world and into the mystical world where my soul resides. In this world, I am a wise and eternal soul, and my purpose is foremost. My personality is always being led forward and urged to express my underlying magnificence. Time after time I am being nudged into wakefulness by events that I have mistaken for happenstance.

That illusion is as it must be, for I was given freewill to discover this for myself. I was given choice as to when and if I would awaken to the truth that I am no mere mortal but one with God living in disguise. I have been unconsciously causing my own victimization with my thoughts, feelings and beliefs about myself and my world.

My personality is waking up, and I am becoming aware that what is speaking into my life is not the mundane sound of a meaningless world but the voice of my own soul, the sound of my authentic self, becoming more familiar.

And now I am holding this book in my hands. Now I am paying attention. I am ready to connect the dots between my thoughts, feelings and beliefs, and the resulting experiences. By connecting the dots of my experiences, I will begin to realize that I have always been conversing with God.

I am now ready for a new definition of God that makes sense to me. I am willing to lean in and listen deeply to my own story. I know that I will find that all of my dots, all of my experiences, will lead me directly to my God.

* * * * * * *

———————————

"Every man is a divinity in disguise,
a god playing the fool."
— Ralph W. Emerson
May 25, 1803 – April 27, 1882

———————————

Chapter 2
The Path from Whys to Wise

As you begin the journey of using your own life to discover God, you will soon encounter a common roadblock; it is the pervasive "Why?" Starting at the beginning of your story, you can come up with no rhyme or reason as to why you were born into a certain family dynamic, or why someone left you, hurt you, ignored you or put you in harm's way. So, you turn to this God, the new loving God that you want to trust and ask "Why?" Why did this happen? Why does God allow ongoing dysfunction, hardship, and drama to play out in my life and in the world? Why does God create a life for me that makes me feel so small?

Because of your past, you learned to live under the radar, not wanting to get hurt, not wanting to get hopes up too high. You learned not to trust anyone, not even yourself—not even God. There may be a sadness in your day-to-day living. Watching others that seem to have it all together makes you feel like an outsider. You assume that they know something you don't know, or that God smiled upon them at birth and gave them a much more pleasant beginning. Living in the shame of an unhealthy past, you may have created a "healthy" façade. You go through the motions of appearing to be well-adjusted while feeling as if you have not been given enough love and nourishment to develop a real desire to live.

One of the biggest hurdles you will need to overcome on your spiritual journey is discovering the answers to your "Whys." Without the answers you are merely trying to live up to someone else's interpretation. But you need to be able to interpret your own life.

---

*"We cannot live in a world that is not our own,
in a world that is interpreted for us by others.
An interpreted world is not a home."*
— *Hildegard of Bingen*
September 16, 1098 – September 17, 1179

Looking at it strictly from the viewpoint of the personality, most people cannot find the answers that would make sense of their lives. From this viewpoint your life began at conception, and your arrival here was like stepping into the middle of a nightly dream and not remembering how you got there. The major players, such as your parents and maybe siblings, were already here. Or perhaps you found yourself in the care of someone other than your parents. Whatever the situation, you probably felt you were a "walk-in" to someone else's story. The rules and the family dynamics were already in place, and it was best to learn what they were as quickly as possible. For many, life became about survival, learning to walk on eggshells and avoiding upsets. This feeling that you were a visitor stepping into someone else's territory was the genesis of your people-pleasing social self and the relinquishing of your authentic self.

Making sense of your life requires that you look beyond your family of origin, deeper than your own birth, deeper than your physicality, personality and memory. From this perspective, I invite you to consider the possibility that you are an eternal soul who is very knowledgeable of life on both the spiritual and physical plane and that you chose to come here. If that is the case, then you could see the situation that you were stepping into, and you knew *why* you were stepping into it in advance. You may be upset by this comment saying, "No way did I choose this for myself!" But consider the possibility that beyond this physical body you are indeed an eternal spiritual being. If that is true, then freewill was not something you discovered tucked into your first diaper but instead is something that you had and used before your incarnation.

In order to begin making sense of your life, you will need to push back from the idea of a physical beginning and see yourself as something much greater and more incredible than you ever imagined. When you do that, you will begin to view this lifetime as a mere drop of eternal life. From this perspective, you can ponder the possibility that you are a unique physical expression of something eternal—an aspect of God, expressing in a unique human form. You are an individual expression of God relating to and living within Its own creation. If that is the case, then it would mean that living behind the stories of your personality, behind the scenes of your life, is God…the God you've been searching for.

But why would God choose this life, this beginning? To answer these questions, you must follow the advice of the sages and take the time to "Know thyself."

Emma Curtis Hopkins (1849-1925), an American spiritual author, teacher and influential figure in the New Thought movement, built her life and philosophy upon metaphysical concepts; a belief in a reality beyond what is perceptible to the senses. One of her students, Ernest Holmes, founded a spiritual movement known as Religious Science. Other students of Emma Curtis Hopkins' teachings, Malinda Cramer, Nona L. Brooks and Fannie Brooks went on to establish Divine Science. Neither of these movements is to be confused with Scientology even though they all have the word "science" in them. These New Thought teachers used their own lives as a laboratory. They felt that there were actual spiritual laws in place, also known as Universal Laws, that governed all of our experiences. They closely observed their own lives and the teachings of others and based their beliefs purely on what could be proven in their own experience. They taught and wrote of their findings and invited others to put their New Thought teachings into practice to see if similar results could be achieved. These theologians believed that there was only one Source, one Presence, within all things. They taught that there were definitive Universal Laws in place that anyone could rely on to produce certain results. They believed that any individual could test these concepts in their own life.

I believe that if you are willing, you will soon discover that your life can become your laboratory, and that the spiritual laws, like the Universal Law of Cause and Effect, are indeed as reliable and observable as the physical Law of Gravity.

But in order to test the Universal Laws you must learn what they are. Four of these important laws will be explained in the next chapter. You will also need to gather the material to be tested. This material cannot be just from the time that you began to awaken to spiritual concepts or picked up this book, but also from the time before your consciousness began to awaken. Just as the physical Law of Gravity did not start working when you learned about it in the second grade, the Universal Law of Cause and Effect did not begin working when you first became aware of its existence. Both laws were always impersonally, continuously and reliably doing what they do.

By looking into your past, you can begin a new search for God as a creative energy that has been acting upon the thoughts, feelings and beliefs that your personality held at the time of your experiences. You will be looking for proof that there is a correlation between your inner thoughts and beliefs and your outer experiences. In order to do this, you must begin connecting the dots between who you felt you were at significant times of your life to see if indeed there is a match between the identity that you held and the events that occurred. For example, when I thought I was a victim because of my abusive childhood, I attracted numerous physical and emotional abusers into my adult life. When I finally learned to feel better about myself, the physical abusers disappeared. But the emotional abusers…well, they are a bit harder to see especially if, as a child, you were taught to ignore what was going on right in front of your own eyes.

By answering key questions in this workbook, you will begin to use your own life as a laboratory to discover evidence of the Universal Laws underpinning your past experiences to the thoughts you held about yourself. You will begin your search for this evidence of God with a brand-new definition of God. This God is not a personality made in the image and likeness of man but instead a loving, creative presence and energy that flows through you and as you. This energy is shaped into outer experiences by your thoughts, feelings and beliefs about yourself and the world you live in.

In my personal example above, the *cause* of my experiences was a belief that I was a victim. A victim is someone who feels they have no power to change undesirable circumstances. This belief stemmed from my childhood experiences of being raised by a loveable but often-absent alcoholic father and a "rageaholic" mother. Like most dysfunctional families during that time, no one talked about the pain caused by unhealthy individuals in the family, so I internalized my feelings. As I matured, I still held the fear and hurt of those experiences within me even though my social-self knew how to produce a façade of being happy and having my act together. The truth was that I did not *feel* that I had my act together. As a matter of fact, I felt like damaged goods. The creative energy, God, ignored my manufactured façade and worked through my underlying identity of victim, and I found myself attracting and attracted to individuals who eventually turned out to be my next abuser. Those abusive relationships were merely the *effect* of my belief that I had been and was still a victim of a painful childhood. Using my own life as a laboratory, I found that as I changed my identity from victim to one who has the power to choose, my relationships changed. Today there is no doubt in my mind that there was a connection between who I believed myself to be and the people and experiences I attracted into my life.

Once I grew into a deeper understanding of myself, everyone and everything in my life changed. I now know why I was born into the family dynamic that was my childhood. All the hurt, blame and shame are gone, because I *know* that on a soul level, I chose my particular set of parents and the accompanying experiences to do the work that I came here to do.

When you discover that there is a connection between who you believed yourself to be during various stages of your life, and the types of people and experiences you attracted into your life at those times, you will be well on your way to finding your answers to "Why."

So many people like to say, "It's all God," but they fail to include themselves in that description. Instead, they hold themselves separate from God and believe that they are merely physical beings that have somewhere within their physicality a soul. But I believe that we are all spiritual beings, individual expressions of God, souls that have put on a "body suit" in order to have a physical experience. Just as our clothes are animated when we are within them but lose their life when we drop them to the floor, so does the body lose its life when the soul no longer animates it. At some point we will all drop the physical body, but what we accomplished here and the essence of what we really are will continue on and on, because what we are is eternal, and the energy we bring into this world continues on after our physical existence. So, in reality, there is no beginning and no end to what you are. Your soul holds the body you use until it lets it go.

If you discover in the course of reading this book that you have indeed been living under spiritual laws, Universal Laws, then that must be because you are a spiritual being and part of the Universe. When you understand that you are a spiritual being, then you can begin to edit your old victim story and replace it with your true identity as an eternal being stepping into the physical realm.

My "Whys" to being born into my family are now clear to me, and I use it in my work. You will soon discover your "Whys" and see that they are gifts waiting to be opened and used by you. Your "Whys" contain your purpose. Your soul is waiting for you to awaken, connect the dots and discover who you are. It is ready for you to discover the creative energy, the presence of God within you, that is shaping your thoughts, feelings and beliefs into your experiences.

"Never the spirit was born,
the spirit shall cease to be never.
Changeless the spirit remains,
birthless and deathless forever."
— Emma Curtis Hopkins
September 2, 1849 – April 25, 1925

You may find it is difficult for your personality to wrap its mind around the idea of an eternal self, but your mind can and will expand to a better understanding if you choose it. You may not have all the answers, but you will have the ones you need to make sense of your life. The answers to all of your questions lie within you, within your life. Connecting the dots between your inner world and your outer experiences is a powerful vehicle for introducing your personality to your authentic self.

This process and the exercises in this book are about being completely honest with yourself. You will have to be willing to let your well-built façade and old stories dissolve so that you can open up to the possibility that God is, and has always been, expressing through you as a projection of your thoughts, feelings and beliefs—as your experiences.

The urges you have to create and express in certain ways, your dreams, your desires, the things you love to do, are your unique God-self pressing upon your personality, attempting to awaken you and express fully through you. Following your heart's desires allows you the experience of merging your God-self with your physical existence. Your own physicality is God touching Its own physical creations.

You see, in spirit form there is no separation between you and your desires. There are no emotions. There is no fear or guilt, and instead of feeling love, you *are* love. This is not a lack of anything; it is just a different state of being. God expressing in the physical, as you or a blade of grass or a butterfly, is the way of God. God is the Creator, the Creative Action and the Creation. It is all God...including you.

This is not to say that your personality, your ego, is God. Your personality's view is capable of ongoing change because it is not real. Your personality is based on your past experiences and the stories that it believed about those experiences. It changes as your perspective changes and can take on new identities. Truth, on the other hand, does not change. God is the constant creative presence, intelligence, cause and source of all things.

Your soul is the individual expression of that presence, and it desires to be free. At any time, you are either allowing it the freedom to fully express in your life, or you are unconsciously blocking it and living purely from the perspective of the personality. When you begin to grasp what you really are, then you will be able to begin the process of releasing resentment and fear. You will then be open to living an authentic life, loving who you are and what you do.

———————————

"The effect of living within a society
oftentimes confuses and complicates
our stream of thought.
It makes people forget who they really are
by causing them to be obsessed
with what they are not."
— Lao-Tzu
604 BC – 531 BC

———————————

* * * * * * *

Chapter 3
The Laws of the Universe

Most people would agree that there are physical laws in place that we have learned to live with, count on and respect. A great example is the Law of Gravity. You know that if you were to jump off a cliff, gravity would pull you downward until you met with another object like, let's say, the ground. Also, we do not hold onto handrails when climbing the stairs because we fear that we will float upwards; we use the handrail to help pull ourselves up against the force of gravity which is pulling us toward the earth's magnetic center. So, we all agree that the Law of Gravity exists. It exists, we respect it, and we use it to our benefit. We make decisions on how we will build things, navigate, irrigate, etc., using this law. We know that the law does not adapt to us, we adapt to it. We know that it is unchangeable, impersonal, reliable and constant.

Also, thanks to Newton, we know that there are laws concerning motion. These laws are also impersonal, reliable and constant. In the first example of jumping off a cliff, we would find ourselves operating under two laws in the same experience; the Law of Gravity and the Law of Motion.

This commingling of laws is also commonly experienced with the Universal Laws. They too are unchangeable, impersonal, reliable and constant. But most people are not even aware that these laws exist because the effect of working against these laws is not as immediate or apparent as the physical laws.

Learning about and understanding these Universal Laws will help you to discover the answers to the "Whys" of your life. Recognizing that you are a spiritual being having a human experience is the first step toward better understanding. Moving into alignment with your true nature, your spiritual nature, allows you to work naturally and effortlessly with these laws just as your physical nature works naturally and effortlessly with the physical laws.

Just as you accept that what goes up must come down, you will also come to understand that what you send out into the world must come back to you. Because these laws are not common knowledge and part of our standardized schooling, we must learn about them through our experiences. This is no accident. This life is your classroom and "When the student is ready, the teacher will appear." This is not an external teacher, but one that is within you, waiting for you to recognize that it has been guiding you along the way from experience to experience throughout your life. Are you, the student, ready to allow your inner teacher to lift you up from where you have been living?

Recognizing and understanding these Universal Laws will allow you to view your past from a new perspective, a higher perspective, and your past will begin to make sense. As you connect the dots of your life, you will begin to understand why things happened and how they couldn't have turned out any other way. There are numerous Universal Laws. In this book, we will look at four of them. Let's start with what I consider to be the most important Universal Law, the one that asks the poignant question, "Who are you?"

* * * * * * * *

The Law of Identity

"As I let go of what I am, I become what I might be."
— Lao Tzu
604 BC – 531 BC

I start with the Law of Identity because if you can discover and live from the truth of who you *really* are, everything else will fall into place. This law acts like an umbrella. It is all-encompassing. Right now, you are moving around in the world holding a view of yourself based on who you think and feel you are. Your experiences, relationships, health, bank account, etc., are matching that identity. If I asked you to describe who you believe yourself to be, and you were perfectly honest, you would begin to see the fingerprints of the Law of Identity in your life. This law also helps to explain why you had the experiences you had in the past.

I like to compare the Law of Identity to a fast-food menu. Identities come with corresponding experiences just as Meal #1 comes with a hamburger, fries and a medium drink. The most common identities that form when operating strictly from the viewpoint of the personality are victim, abuser and rescuer. These three identities are co-dependent, meaning that they are dependent upon each other for their existence. You can't have an abuser without a victim. You also cannot have a rescuer without a victim and an abuser. Each one plays off the other.

The identity of "Victim" for example comes with abusers, rescuers, poor health, a lot of drama and a dwindling bank account. All people who feel they are a victim of someone or something, have similar experiences. Common battle cries of this identity are, "Why is this always happening to me?" or "It's so unfair!" They often use the word "they" to describe what is going on in their lives because it seems as if someone from the outside is always doing something to them.

I know this well because I was once a member of this group. Because of what "they," my parents, had done to me, I held hurt and shame deep inside me and carried it with me wherever I went. Others could not see it but at the very core of my being, I felt I was a victim of a painful childhood.

I didn't know about the Law of Identity at the time but looking back at my early relationships and experiences I can now see they made perfect sense for the identity of Victim. A victim can't be a victim without an abuser. So, I had my abuser, and was living in debt, subsidized housing, emotional pain and fear. I still had my health because I was in my twenties, but I doubt I would have had it for very long since I was being tossed across the room by my partner on a regular basis. It took me 6½ years and multiple bruises before I decided I deserved better, upgraded my sense of identity and found the courage to leave.

But the Law of Identity is not about blame. In fact, it is not about the other person at all. It is about us. The feelings we have about ourselves create our sense of identity, and that identity comes with a package deal of corresponding people and experiences. The good news is that we have freewill and we can use it to change our minds about who we think and feel we are. Today, thinking and feeling differently about who and what I am, I have attracted people and experiences into my life that are tremendously different from those in the past and make perfect sense for my present identity. You see, any shift in your identity, in your "I am-ness," automatically creates a change in your experiences. It's the Law.

I'll never forget sitting in my kitchen on my fortieth birthday, having wine with a friend, and once again lamenting my childhood and the diminished experience of life I thought I would always have because of my parents. My friend surprised me when he said, "Are you finished with that story?" I was in shock and more than a little miffed that he was minimizing my painful and very true story. But after he left, I sat and pondered what he said. It was so powerful. It never occurred to me until that moment that you could be finished with a story.

Most of us do not realize that we are all living within our stories, and that we can be finished with one and move on to another. We can drop it, edit it, create a new slant and even use it to help others. But whatever we decide to do, when it changes, and we change our sense of identity, everything begins to change.

We are all here moving through identities with the potential to travel from a sense of victimhood to true empowerment. How do you know which identity you are currently working from—victim, rescuer, abuser or empowered one? Look at your relationships and experiences. Do you find yourself in similar predicaments or patterns even though the other players change? The first thing to do is realize that *you* are the common denominator. Describe the experiences and how you feel about what "they" are doing to you or to someone else and there is your identity. Are "they" keeping you from your best life?

As you become more aware of what is really going on, you will begin to see that your own unpleasant experiences and patterns are nothing more than a projection of your sense of identity. These experiences also serve as an ongoing invitation for you to choose something better for yourself; to love yourself more. "They" provided a crossroad so that you could decide if you would continue on with your current identity and experiences or say that you've had enough. "They" kept coming in many forms until one of them became your perfect last straw.

When you see that, you will see that those you felt were your nemesis actually served to move you along your path toward self-love and true empowerment. With this insight you can choose to let them off the hook and free yourself of a lifetime of resentment. This shift in perspective will also free up a tremendous amount of physical, mental and emotional energy so that you can begin to make better choices for yourself. Your new choices will cause the old patterns to crumble and a new identity with its corresponding experiences to emerge.

With new eyes, you will be able to see that everyone is on their own journey moving through different identities, each receiving personal invitations to step closer to their truth, to true empowerment. You will begin to respect, not interfere, with others on their own sacred journeys. With healthy boundaries in place, safe and mutually supportive relationships can develop, and the quality of your life will begin to change dramatically. With each healthy choice, you will gain access to a new level of self-confidence, self-love, awareness, understanding and authentic power.

Remember the Law of Identity is not about blame, but instead it is about discovering what identity is at the root of your experiences. The reason that similar scenarios appear in your life is because your identity, who you think and feel you are, determines your experiences. A person who feels that they are a victim of anything or anyone, will attract experiences that validate that identity no matter how many times they move, change jobs or change relationships.

"Believe as though you are, and you will be."
— Ernest Holmes
January 21, 1887 – April 7, 1960

As you begin to look more closely at your life, you will discover that the answer has always been "Yes" to whatever you think, feel and believe about yourself. If you think that you are a victim of the government, a partner, a sibling, a parent—it doesn't really matter—you will be justified in your description of yourself. Even the Bible says, "By your words you are justified; by your words you are condemned." You will always be justified. You will always be proven right. There is no "other" doing this to you. Because the Law of Identity is impersonally supporting your notion of who you believe yourself to be, you sit right in the middle of your experiences creating them with your thoughts, feelings and beliefs.

On the other hand, if you believe you are an eternal soul, a creator, made in the image and likeness of God, and that you have control over your personality's thoughts and experiences, you will also be justified in that description. When you awaken to the truth that you are no mere mortal but a personality partnering with a powerful creator, creating with your thoughts, feelings and beliefs, you will become aware of your own God-given powers and aware of God in action. In this moment, you can begin to look at your past and present experiences and realize that you have been working under this reliable law all along.

This law also explains why you may feel as if some of your "prayers" are not answered. In truth, you have already been given everything. What you desire is only waiting for you to show up as a match to it.

When I felt I was a victim, I could not attract what I desired to experience in my life. I was not a match for all the good that was available to me. I could only attract the little that made sense for my identity. To begin receiving my good I had to learn to love myself and know that I was good. I had to upgrade my identity. When I did, I did not have to pray or plead for my good, it came running to meet me because it was a match for my upgraded identity. So many people walk around feeling that they are innately bad and that they are sinners. They limp through life accepting the crumbs of others until they choose another identity, another way of seeing themselves.

Remember the tests in grade school where you were given two columns and asked to match up the description with the correct answer? That is how this law works. Until you become a match for your desire, you do not see it in your life. The answers to your prayers, your desires, are you.

They are waiting for you to show up as a match to them. You don't get what you desire in this life, you get who and what you feel you *are*.

———————————

"What you think, you become. What you feel, you attract.
What you imagine, you create."
— Gautama Buddha
Approx. 563 BC – 483 BC

———————————

Try the following matching exercise to see if you are beginning to grasp how the Law of Identity works. Draw a dotted line, connecting the dots between who a person feels they are and how their life might look with that identity. You are practicing connecting the dots between an "I am" belief and possible outcomes.

"And God said to Moses, I AM THAT I AM..."
Law of Identity Quiz

1. I am a survivor; I persevere.

2. I am an unlimited spiritual being.

3. I am very likely to inherit all the diseases that run in my family.

4. I come from a very dysfunctional family. I am damaged goods.

5. I am the only one that sees clearly. Others are so stupid!

6. I am good at rescuing others.

7. I am stuck in a lousy job market.

8. I am in love with life!

9. I am a worthless sinner.

10. I am living in a loving and mutually supportive world.

A. An abundant, unlimited life

B. Arguments and debates; a life filled with conflicts

C. Co-dependent relationships

D. Genetic diseases

E. One challenge after another

F. A life of guilt; fear of God

G. Surrounded by loving and supportive people

H. Unhealthy relationships or no relationship

I. Unemployed or underemployed

J. A full and joyful life

Don't worry if you didn't get all of them correct. This is just an exercise to play with the "I Am" in a non-personal, non-judgmental way. If you want to, you could now try connecting the dots between your past thoughts, feelings and beliefs about yourself and see if any of them were a match to your experience. What was your experience as a child? What was your experience in high school? What was your experience in your 30s? If you find that there is a match between your experiences and how you felt about yourself, you will begin to see the Law of Identity operating in your own life. Know that this law, like the Law of Gravity, is always working impersonally and consistently. Know also that you are always loved and supported in your journey toward growth and understanding.

Answers:
1.E., 2.A., 3.D., 4.H., 5.B., 6.C., 7.I., 8.J., 9.F., 10.G.

Also, don't be concerned if you don't feel that you live the majority of your time in the identity of an empowered one. Most of us don't. We catch glimpses of something acting through our thoughts, feelings and beliefs, and begin to grasp that there is more going on within us, but then get caught up in life and find ourselves in situations that we don't remember choosing. Luckily, there is more than one Universal Law working in our lives at all times and they serve to wake us up whenever we fall asleep to who we really are. Whether you are experiencing something that you enjoy, or something that you disdain, there is always a cause. Actually, there are two causes:

1. Original Cause—God—pure creative energy acting upon...
2. Your "I Am" thoughts, feelings and beliefs—your identity

I still catch myself occasionally slipping back into victimhood. Remember that this journey is about moving from victimhood to empowerment. So, be gentle with yourself. Don't become your own abuser. Whenever I begin to feel that something or someone else is unfair, and I want others to agree with me and fight for me, I know that I have slipped back into some form of victimhood.

The solution is always the same; become completely honest with myself and ask myself the hard questions. Did I enter into this situation or relationship for the right reasons? Was I feeling empty or alone? Did I override the voice of my inner guidance and choose something that was not a good fit for me? Was I trying to prove something or get something? If the answer is yes to any of these, then I can hardly call myself a victim.

Your authentic self, who you really are, is your only path to true empowerment and connection. You are an individual and unique expression of God, and when you allow yourself to discover your own natural interests and talents, you move closer to discovering God. All the support you need is waiting for you. All your good is waiting for you to become a match to it.

———————

"Claim your divine, glorious selfhood. Think it, talk it,
live it and it will demonstrate itself in your life."
— Emmet Fox
July 30, 1886 – August 13, 1951

———————

* * * * * * *

The Law of Cause and Effect

Many people have heard of this law. It may have been presented as, "Do unto others as you would have them do unto you." Some people refer to it as the Law of Karma. This law is a wonderful teacher of compassion and personal responsibility. It is the great equalizer. It works in the positive and the negative. Since most people are not walking around questioning why so much good is coming into their life, we'll look at an example of this law from the flip side.

If you take something from someone, something will be taken from you. If someone takes something from you, something will be taken from them, and they will feel the same discomfort that they inflicted on you. The same individuals might not be involved, but everything will be brought back into balance. This law is where justice lives. So, if you feel someone has taken your good, you can let go of your desire to punish or get revenge and rely on this law. This law will always bring everything back into order. Your good will be returned to you, but it is very likely that it will not happen in the same timeframe, or possibly even involve the same individual(s). That is why we so often miss the original cause of our more challenging life experiences. But if we begin to pay attention and connect the dots, we will learn to trust that this law will bring everything back into perfect balance at the perfect time.

It is very important to remember to work with the Universal Laws; they are always in place and are consistent and impersonal. If someone has taken something from you, and you *do* decide to hold a grudge or desire to punish them and hold resentment toward them, then you are setting yourself up for another to do the same to you. If you think that you have forgiven someone, like an old boyfriend, but you still want their good withheld from them by the Universe, that could be the very reason you experience a lack of flow in your own life. I know that forgiving and wishing someone the best can be a tall order, especially if you feel they have caused you a lot of pain, but when we open our minds to the lessons of this powerful law, we see that we are being guided to *really* understand that we are one. What we "do unto others, we do unto ourselves."

Working with this law means putting yourself in another's place. Always ask yourself if what you are about to do to another is something you would like to experience yourself. Just know that if your answer is "yes," and you do it, you will get an opportunity to find out if your choice was a good one because it will be done to you.

You see these laws work in the positive and the negative. If you are kind, others will be kind to you. If you are giving, others will be generous toward you. If you are grateful, you will receive more to be grateful about. If you are judgmental, you will be judged. If you take something from another, something will be taken from you. If you block another's good, your good will be blocked.

This law may sometimes feel like a blessing and sometimes like a punishment. In reality, it is impersonal. Its demonstration does teach us compassion. It does teach us to love our neighbor as ourselves. It does teach us personal responsibility for our actions. We begin to understand that the God within all is not rewarding us or punishing us for our deeds. Instead, we discover that for every action there is an equal reaction. This law is nudging us into alignment with our true nature. We get to choose the thought and the action with our free will. The Law of Cause and Effect does the rest. No punishment. No blessing. Just choice.

Look at the questions below regarding the Law of Cause and Effect in your own life. See if you can find a correlation.

1. Can you think of an experience in your past that would serve as an example of the Law of Cause and Effect at work in your life?

2. Is there anything you are involved in right now where this law might make you consider a different approach to the situation?

Following are some affirmations to help you work with this law to produce positive outcomes:

<u>Affirmations</u>

I know that what I truly am cannot be harmed by another personality.

I am a soul, an individual expression of God.

One soul cannot harm another soul. We are one and the same.

We are all in the process of discovering our true nature.

We are all learning about the laws through our experiences.

I am gentle with myself and others on this journey of Self-discovery.

I live in a mutually supportive universe.

I am ready to let go of all resentment toward others.

I release them and wish them the very best on their journey.

I know that my good will always be restored to me. It is the law.

I see nothing but good for all of us.

* * * * * * *

The Law of Reciprocity

There are differing explanations of this law, but the element that they all have in common is that what you send out comes back to you—like a boomerang. This law deals with the feeling, the vibration, that you are sending out into the world. You are operating at various times of the day at different emotional levels that literally affect your physical energy, mental clarity and experiences. For instance, you may start out your day feeling grumpy about what you have to do, and then as the day wears on you may find yourself getting angrier and angrier and begin experiencing conflicts with other individuals or with your computer. Later in the day you may stop, get centered and feel gratitude. If you pay attention, you will feel the shift in your physical energy, mental clarity and your experiences. These feelings have very different vibrations. Stepping into gratitude makes you feel energized, and your life seems to move into a nice flow. Being grumpy makes you feel drained and leaves you bumping into one obstacle after another.

You may not realize it, but when you begin your day in a low vibration you are not having a private experience, but instead you are sending that out into your universe. Your universe then sends low vibration experiences back to you. Just like gravity, it does not do that to punish, it does that because that's what it does. It does that because it is responding to your feelings. In this case, it might look like lost keys, a traffic jam, a flat tire, a rude driver, etc.; anything that would keep most anybody grumpy. It sends any experience that matches the energy that you sent out into its ethers.

"You will not be punished for your anger,
you will be punished by your anger."
— *Gautama Buddha*
Approx. 563 BC – 483 BC

But if at any time during the above challenges, you were able to get centered, and put things in perspective, you would realize that the Law of Reciprocity was doing what it does. You could then choose to change up the energy by focusing on all the things that are working in your life. Calming yourself and telling yourself during a traffic jam that everything is unfolding perfectly, you would then be feeling more at peace and sending out a higher vibration into the Universe. The Universe would reciprocate in like experiences; for instance, you end up having a meaningful conversation on the elevator that would not have happened had you arrived earlier.

You are pure creative energy, and this law teaches you to manage that energy. You are the stuff of God. If you pay attention, you will feel in your body the energy that is being produced by your thoughts, feelings and beliefs. Depending on what you are internalizing, you are operating somewhere within a range of high to low level vibration.

On the following pages you will find examples of high and low levels of thoughts and feelings and corresponding vibrational experiences and suggestions for managing your emotions and energy.

Examples of High and Low Level Thoughts and Feelings

Low Level	High Level
Guilt	Compassion for Yourself
Fear	Trust in the support of the Universe
Overwhelmed	Peaceful and Centered
Critical	Accepting
Judgmental	Compassionate
Negative	Optimistic
Jealous	Mutually Supported
Depressed	Grateful
Trapped	Free
Shame	Self-love

Examples of Corresponding Vibrational Experiences

Low Level	High Level
Poor Health	Good Health
Lack of Energy	Strength & Vitality
Repeated Victimization	Healthy Relationships
Accidents	Meaningful Coincidences
Debt	Abundance/Opportunities
Loneliness	Awareness of Inner Connection

Keep in mind that the low and high-level examples of experiences shown are not punishments or blessings. They are simply matches for differing vibrations. You can see the benefits of doing the spiritual work to consciously manage our emotions instead of letting them manage us.

Suggestions for Dramatically Changing Up Your Vibration/Energy

- Drop the manipulators, energy vampires and toxic individuals from your life.
- Turn off the negative news and conversations.
- Stop negative trains of thought and switch to knowledge of God's unending support.
- Discover and follow your passion.
- Do service-oriented work that you love.
- Live in integrity; *be* what you say you believe.
- Meditate.
- Contemplate that you are a spiritual being /one with God/one with all.
- Keep a gratitude journal.
- Choose supportive friends.
- Spend time with like-minded individuals to discuss your spiritual nature.
- Expose yourself to positive stories/films/songs, etc.
- Choose your good/visualize your best life/consciously create.

- Move your body—dance/exercise/stretch.

- Spend time in nature.

- Listen to your favorite music.

- Spend time getting to know yourself.

- Be compassionate and gentle with yourself.

- Take your inner child on play dates to the zoo, a movie, etc.

- Whatever makes you happy and feel good about yourself and this world…do that!

————————

"When you arise in the morning,
think of what a precious privilege it is to be alive—
to breathe, to think, to enjoy, to love."
— Marcus Aurelius
April 26, 121 AD – March 17, 180 AD

————————

* * * * * * * *

The Law of Attraction

"Our thought is the unseen magnet,
ever attracting its correspondence in things seen and tangible."
— Prentice Mulford
April 5, 1834 – May 27, 1891

This law teaches us that we bring into our lives whatever we focus our attention on. We attract into our lives what we spend our time thinking about. Thoughts are things. Many people have heard this but don't necessarily believe it. If we are thinking about our lack of health, relationship, funds, or our bills, poor job and housing markets, etc., we will magnetize more of those experiences into our lives. The creative energy of the Universe goes to work on what we have given it in the way of our thoughts. *It* gives energy to what *we* are giving our energy to—like attracts like. We are a team! So, what do you spend most of your time thinking about? To what are you giving a lot of your attention?

If you saw your mind as a powerful magnifying glass and knew your thoughts about a particular concern are being enlarged by this magnifying glass, you would realize that your concerns and challenges are out of proportion to everything else that is going on in your life. These concerns seem to take on a life of their own. Unfortunately, it is your life that is being consumed by the thoughts. Since it is the thing that you are giving the largest percentage of your attention to, you will soon notice that there are more experiences similar to your original concern gravitating toward you.

A very common example is debt. When someone finds themselves in debt, it is because they are working through one of the previous laws. Perhaps they wished another person ill, believed on some level that money is the root of all evil, or couldn't see themselves as financially successful. Another possibility is that they believed everything they heard in the news regarding the status of the economy. Debt doesn't appear out of the clear blue. It is the result of thoughts, feelings and beliefs. Once it shows up in our life, though, it has a way of getting a huge amount of our attention. That is perfectly understandable because we live in a society based on money, and the lack of it produces fear. We all know that we need money to pay our bills, buy necessities, etc.

Unaware of the Law of Attraction, one could find themselves falling deeper and deeper into debt. More bills seem to come in every day. The car needs a new transmission, medical bills mount up, credit card companies increase their rates, etc., It may feel as if this is just a string of bad luck, but that is not true. There is no such thing as bad luck or good luck. There are Universal Laws that work 100% of the time, and, in this case, focusing on lack enacts the Law of Attraction and brings more lack. Remember, lack is just one example of a thought that we may be magnifying.

The solution is to take our mind off of the problem and put it on what we do want to see in our lives. But trying to take your mind off of lack, when you feel like you are in the midst of it and debt collectors are calling, is indeed difficult. It requires a Herculaneum effort to begin to think of something else, but you can do it! Actually, you must do it to affect a change in your experiences.

First, think of what you would love...not what you would *like* but what you would *love*. Love is a very powerful word. Stand in front of a mirror and practice saying something that you would like in your life. Now replace it with what you would *love*. Did you notice the difference in your body language? That is because you are speaking God's language.

48

Love calling Love. The word *love* says to the Universe that you are completely on board. In this case, you might say, "I would *love* to be financially flush!" Now visualize yourself going to the bank to deposit money into an already full checking account. Imagine writing the final check to one of your current billers and adding "Thank You" in the memo, grateful for the use of their money. Imagine putting a stamp on the envelope and dropping it into the mailbox. Imagine the next statement that says balance due $0. Now imagine where you would *love* to travel or what you would *love* to do next.

Second, sit in gratitude for all of the abundance already in your life. Yes, you have a ton of riches in your life! Can you write? Can you read? Do you know how many people cannot read or write? Do you have fingers, legs, arms? Do you know how to drive? Do you have your eyesight? These may not seem like riches because you have taken these incredible gifts for granted, but I guarantee that if you offered someone the ability to walk or a pile of money, they would quickly choose the former. Sitting in gratitude for everything you have, focuses your attention on abundance. The Law of Attraction will draw experiences to you that match that feeling of abundance.

Remember, the Universe is not rewarding you or punishing you, it is simply following your thoughts. It is always matching experiences to your thoughts whether they are ones of lack or abundance. It is saying "Yes," to whatever you are thinking.

Be very careful not to outline how or when a change will appear. *This is so important.* Do not think about the amount that you desire, only that it be so much that you never have to worry about, in this case, money again. Aaaaah, doesn't that feel good? Also, do not think about *how* the money comes to you. When you outline, you are getting into the "how" and that is God's territory. Leave the "how" to the infinite intelligence and divine coordination of God. When you outline or try to control the timing and the possible ways that you can experience abundance, you are actually standing in your own way.

Instead, realize that God did not create lack or have a desire for you to experience it. God did not create the human experience so that we could spend all of our time worrying about money, relationships, jobs, etc. God is abundance and infinite possibilities, and there is no limit to the ways that our good can come to us. There is also no limit to the amount of good we can receive unless we put a cap on it.

Recognize that we are the ones with the hang-ups about money, not God. We are the ones who think that money is one of the big things, the more challenging things, to manifest. To God, All That Is, money is just one more form of Its own energy expressing. Actually, money is often just a barometer of how much good (God) we feel we deserve to receive.

Eventually, you will not even have to think of the issue and what you want. Instead, when something seems to go amiss you can go immediately to God. Just contemplating what God is and what you are can change up the outcome of any situation. In that contemplation you will find within yourself the answers to what is really going on for you. For most of us, it is just that we are so confused about who and what we are, what God is, and how all of this works.

One analogy that my students have felt provided clarity on what God is, is that of an overhead projector. For those of you that do not remember this precursor to power point, it is basically a light box that allows you to lay transparencies that contain text upon a light. That light then projects whatever is written onto a large screen. I suggested that they allow themselves to imagine God as that light, as a pure creative loving energy, projecting through their thoughts and into their world. I reminded them that they possessed the freewill to decide for themselves which transparencies—which thoughts, feelings and beliefs—they would lay upon the Light of God, but whatever they chose would be projected into their life.

When you really think about it, our thoughts are transparent. They really are nothingness. You can't touch thoughts, but if you pay attention you will see that they can and do project themselves into your life when you attach feelings to them. But by what means? I am sure that you agree that you have thoughts but *what* gives them the energy to create your experiences? Is this not the pure creative energy of God creating through your thoughts?

One important goal of this book is to see if you can find God in the midst of your life. One way to test this theory of God as pure creative energy, as pure Light projecting through your thoughts, feelings and beliefs, is to look at what you have created so far. By looking at your past and present experiences you can see if what you have consciously or subconsciously laid upon the light, upon God, was in some way projected into your life. If you find that you have been living in a projection of what you thought, felt and believed, then you have found God in your life. Not the judgmental God of the old stories but a loving God, allowing you to exercise your freewill and write your own stories.

1. What have you been focusing your attention on lately?

2. What experiences in your life do you think could be the result of your focus on positive thoughts?

3. What experiences in your life do you think could be the result of your focus on negative thoughts?

4. Have you been trying to manage your challenges instead of changing the negative thoughts that created the challenges?

5. Are you ready to replace the negative thoughts with new empowering thoughts?

* * * * * * *

Chapter 4
The Journey of the Soul

You can probably relate to some of the mortification and devastation that Steve Jobs, founder and CEO of Apple Computer, was feeling when he was handed his walking papers by the board of the very company that he and Steve Wozniak had started. Perhaps you have found yourself being openly fired or humiliated in some way in your life. Many people have been surprised to learn that their partner is having an affair, or that their boss was planning to fire them, only to find out later that everyone but them could read the writing on the wall. In any case, it is natural to feel betrayed by the friends and coworkers that remained silent.

Perhaps you once felt similarly betrayed and wondered how you would ever get over it. Better yet, did you ever get over it? Many people spend the rest of their lives reliving an event that lasted only a few moments. Certainly, an event like this can bring anyone to their emotional knees, but for some reason many stay down while some get up. Steve Jobs got up and later connected the dots.

In a commencement address at Stanford University on June 12, 2005, Steve Jobs shared that being fired from Apple was one of the best things that ever happened to him. He felt the weight of being successful was lifted, and he felt free to begin again. He then entered into one of the most creative periods of his life.

Upon reflection, Steve Jobs was able to see that he had been feeling the "heaviness" of being successful. Even though he had not consciously set out to get himself fired, I suggest that he played a big part in his own dismissal. With thought, he could see that the dismissal, even with public humiliation, something our ego dreads, was a very good thing.

––––––––––––

"Thought is creative, and the more emotional the thought, the more creative it is. It is not because we have contemplated and meditated and prayed and fasted; our thought is creative because that is our nature. Our nature is God, and the nature of God does not change."
—Ernest Holmes, founder of Religious Science
January 21, 1887 – April 7, 1960

––––––––––––

You see the Universal Laws, as discussed in the last chapter, follow your true feelings. Feelings override your conscious thoughts. That is why affirmations alone do not work. Affirmations without compatible feelings are only empty words. Feelings even override your rational thoughts. If you've ever been in love and lost someone close to you, you know what I mean. Whether you ended the relationship, or someone else made the decision, if you still have strong feelings for the other person, despite your rational thoughts, you are tied to them and will find it almost impossible to move on.

It is not until you are able to feel that there is something more for you that the strings will dissolve and that something more can come in.

In Steve Jobs' case, he felt that there was something more to do. Letting go of the old was the only way it could come in but come in it would. If the feeling of being trapped is strong enough, your soul will find a way to set itself free. Whatever the obstacle, it *will* be moved. It will either give way by the action you choose to take, or it is taken away, but in the end, it must always move out of the way.

This is going on all around you. If you stand still for a minute, you will see this dynamic at play everywhere in every life. Many people complain day after day about their jobs, looking forward to the weekends and dreading the next week, but then are completely shocked when they are laid off, laid-up, fired or the company closes. That dread, that desire to not be there, is a powerful force. Most of us just don't realize that what we feel is projected into our experiences. We think we can internalize our feelings, that we can play a game on our authentic selves. Many invest their time and energy creating a façade that would fool anyone, even themselves...but not your heart and certainly not your soul. Heart and soul are waiting to unite with our minds, but if we are insistent upon silencing and negating their voices, they will make themselves known through our physical experiences.

Whatever it is that you are feeling will be out-pictured into your life. If you are feeling inadequate, you will attract people or situations that will reinforce that feeling. If you are feeling hopeful, you will encounter stories and opportunities that present you with the possibility of a new life.

We all have feelings churning inside of us, a sea of emotions. We may be feeling positive then suddenly insecure, scared or confused because of something that happened. It is a common human condition. I use the phrase "sea of emotions" because water represents our emotions. Tears are shed when we are both happy and sad.

The Bible offers a wonderful parable of how to deal with our emotions when they get out of control. Look more closely at Luke's story about Jesus calming the storm. A storm erupts while Jesus is sailing with his disciples to the "other side." We might think of our own minds as the vessel being tossed about by all the emotions that come its way. We can relate to the fear that the disciples felt, longing to feel the relief of already being on the "other side" of the situation. That is what it feels like to be out of touch with the truth of our soul. This story shows us how even our own fears have purpose and can cause us to wake up to the teacher within. It shows how your soul, your authentic self, can rock the boat of the façade that you have created. Jesus calming the sea isn't a story of how to command the winds and water, but instead, how to calm our emotions with Truth, and move into sync with our souls. When we replace fearful thoughts with Truth spoken into our minds by our inner teacher, we awaken ourselves to our higher consciousness and are able to calm our personalities with deeper understanding.

It is in the remembering that we are not mere mortals but individual expressions of God, with wonderful Universal Laws, reliable as gravity, at work in our lives, that calms our emotions and allow us to once again sail smoothly through life. Remembering our truth allows us to transition from one state of consciousness to another, from fear to trust. The parable of Jesus calming the storm illustrates us falling asleep to our own higher consciousness. The water represents our emotions, creating what appears to be a dangerous situation or unnecessary drama when our personality is left to its own devices. In their fear, the men awaken their Christ (which means enlightened one) consciousness, their inner teacher, and the waters once again become calm. In our fear, we can reach for something within us, our higher consciousness, our inner teacher, to calm us with Truth. So, you see, even our fear is on purpose and helps us get to the "other side" of whatever story we are living in that is causing us distress.

When we are asleep to the truth of who we are, we often unconsciously choose to do things that scare us or harm us and use them to help ourselves awaken. We marry the wrong person, we take drugs, we drink, we overeat, we become addicted to drama, and we sentence ourselves to jobs and lives that are totally alien to our authentic self, our souls. One day, if we choose to wake up, we realize that our soul is strong, that it has always been at the helm, and it is our choices that have been the rough water on our own journey. We have created the fear with our own thoughts. Some of us may have steered off course so many times that we are finally tiring of a journey to nowhere. We begin to look around for something that makes more sense, something that breaks the cycle. Eventually, if we choose to look, we will find the map written upon our heart and begin to trust it to guide us to our authentic self. We discover that our soul knows where we want to go, and it knows how to get us there. Looking back and charting our lives, we find that our soul, our higher self, has been speaking into our lives all along. It is using whatever life choices we make to move us toward our destination. Nothing has been lost. Everything was on purpose. Everything was used to bring us to this moment.

The soul is not confined by our concepts of space and time. It is never too late. And even if you think you did it wrong, in reality, you did it right. The thing that you are punishing yourself for was very likely a necessary turning point. What you consider to be one of your less than stellar moments, may have been the perfect last straw causing you to discontinue an old way of being. That moment provided the crossroad that allowed you to choose something new. Your belief that you took the wrong path very likely moved you into a position to meet the right person or stand in the perfect spot for what was to happen next.

Still, without a map you might feel lost. Stopping to chart the course of how you got where you are today is a powerful navigational tool for where you are going. Connecting the dots will help you to see the path you have been traveling and the guidance you have been receiving all along. You will discover that you are not alone. You will discover that you can trust, perhaps for the first time in your life, that you are truly loved, guided and supported in becoming your best self. You will discover that you are being led to your good even in the midst of what your personality would call "mistakes" from using its freewill. You will realize that there is no judgment. There is no right or wrong, only attempts to move you toward an understanding of your true nature. You will discover God in the details of your life.

In reality, you have held the map all along. It was written upon your heart before you came into the physical realm, and it has taken you to different ports allowing you to learn experientially your capacity for love and compassion. It has provided you with opportunities to excavate your true divine nature. Through all of it, you have caught glimpses of your authentic self and felt the pull of something that was hidden under the stories that were given to you by others. That pull is the sound of your soul speaking into your heart. Your soul knows where it wants to go and where it yearns to be, and it is the same as what you truly desire beyond your fears. When your heart, mind and soul converge, the journey becomes smooth. You begin to trust that the next step will be provided, the destination will be made clear, and you will find yourself doing what feels right for you. You will also find that you have automatically fallen into alignment with the Laws of the Universe, *your* Universe.

The following are examples of turning points on the journey of individual souls. Do not think that if you are not famous that your journey is less important than another's. Fame is only important to the personality. I've only chosen these very public individuals because we all recognize them and can look at how what initially appeared to be a setback turned into a new way of their being in the world and allowed them to express their unique talents and authentic self.

Turning points on the journey of individuals souls . . .

— **J.K. Rowling,** accused of daydreaming, was fired from her job as a secretary in a busy London office. Using her free time, she created tales of a young wizard named Harry Potter and the rest is history.

— **Mariah Carey** was fired from her job as a hat-check girl at a downtown New York Club in 1988. She began working as a back-up singer for Brenda K. Starr. Since then she has sold millions of albums.

— **Martha Stewart** lost her job as a Wall Street trader after the 1973 recession. She opened a bakery with a friend in Connecticut that grew into a multimillion-dollar business and her life took off. Even with the set-back of a scandal and time served in prison she followed her dream and continued on.

— **Betty Ford** passed away during the writing of this book. When listening to an interview during which she was asked about her own history of addiction she explained that sometimes what we initially think is a negative can become a positive. All the "Whys" can be answered when we stop seeing everything as something that happened *to* us but instead as something that happened *through* us.

Sharing that both her father and brother had been addicted to alcohol, she started a dialogue to discuss the brokenness of her own life and used it to help others. She gave both men and women with an addiction a voice. She went on to open the Betty Ford Clinic which has since become synonymous with rehabilitation. She also shared her diagnosis of breast cancer with the public.

In both cases, there was concern that her honesty would affect the public's opinion toward the First Lady and ultimately, the President. At that time, no one talked openly about their addictions and people diagnosed with cancer whispered the word to very few because of all the fear that surrounded it. To have someone come out so publicly about her addiction and diagnosis of breast cancer was unheard of in the 70s. She gave both addiction and cancer a voice. So many that were hurting and hiding felt that they could finally come out from beneath the stigma attached to these two issues and get the help and support they needed. She gave love and compassion a voice. She made it okay to be real.

So many of us hold our stories so tightly to us and do not realize how common our stories are. We don't see the purpose in bringing the past into the bright light of today. But this one woman allowed her stories to be shared. She re-purposed her life experiences. She used all of her stories. With the dots connected between her past and present experiences, she realized that they were not mistakes but were on purpose. It was what she came here to do. Today people speak much more freely about attending support groups and receiving therapy without the fear of being judged.

There are so many others moving out of the shadows of guilt and shame and sharing their stories. There are so many brave souls in our lifetime willing to move past the cries of their ego, willing to drop the façade of appearing as "normal" as possible. We were given voices and ears for a reason. And we were given hurts and hearts for a reason. We all have planted within us a desire to drop the charade and be authentic for a reason. We came here to make a difference, to break the cycles of abuse and addiction, to remove the stigma around suicide and disease, and to replace judgment of sexual preferences with mutual respect, support and love.

We have chosen to come here as compassionate messengers letting others know that it is alright to come out now, to be who you really are. Imagine the relief when others realize that they are not alone, that they and many others share the same story. The courage and candor of brave souls sends the message to others that it is safe, that it is okay to be yourself.

In truth, the only way to feel closer to God is to be real, is to be yourself, to be *that* unique expression of God. For some it is about exposing what is hidden, for others it is to sing, to write, to cook, to teach, and on and on.

For the longest time, people hid their stories. They were afraid of being alienated by their church, their friends, their work, their families. But living a lie was too painful and they found themselves finally uttering their truth. Most assuredly, living in the aftermath was painful for their personalities. But even in those painful experiences, Truth was being revealed and they were being moved along by their soul, their authentic self.

They discovered that family isn't necessarily the people of their origin; instead it is those with whom your truth is safe. Family is made up of special individuals you choose and who love, respect and support you in living an authentic life. Your true spiritual home doesn't house a judgmental God who sees you as a sinner, but instead is a group of individuals that reflects the divine within you. Your true friends energize you with their presence and they accept and love you for who you are. Your authentic work expresses your unique talents and is a perfect match for who you are. This is what they, and all of us, are discovering on our journey to our authentic selves.

More people are coming out with their truth in our lifetime than ever before. And more families, friends, churches, businesses and governments are questioning whether they need to revise their initial reactions and accept others as they are. Do you see this? Together we are finding that we *can* bear the stories of others, as a matter of fact we've been waiting for the stories, for the truth to be revealed. We can feel the truth soften our hearts and soften our world. We can feel the walls that were constructed by fear fall all around us. All of us benefit when we show up and follow the map that is written upon our hearts and recognize that we are indeed on a journey of the soul. We are traveling together toward a more compassionate world.

We don't remember it, but we signed up for this life and this work, and we are all watching our world change for the better. Just think back to what life was like in the 60s and then look at all the progress that has been made in the world we live in today. LGBTQ+ rights, women's equality, handicap accessibility, interracial marriage, exposure of sexual abuse in our churches, work places, sports and universities, and racial and religious acceptance are just a few of the areas where advancement has been made. So much has happened in such a short amount of time because so many are finding their voice and living from their truth. Connecting our own dots allows us to discover our truth and our own purpose. It is the map written upon our heart by our souls, our authentic selves.

———————————

"Dare to declare who you are. It is not far
from the shores of silence to the boundaries of speech.
The path is not long, but the way is deep. You must not only walk there,
you must be prepared to leap."
— Hildegard of Bingen
September 16, 1098 – September 17, 1179

———————————

* * * * * *

Chapter 5
Finding Your Dots

Your dots are the stories that you tell yourself. They are the thoughts, beliefs and even more importantly, the feelings that you have embraced in the present and held in the past. These dots, these stories, are what you are currently placing and/or have placed upon the light, the creative energy, God. These stories are then projected into your life and into your world. Discovering and following your dots, your thoughts, beliefs and feelings, is the path to discovering God very active and always present in your life.

What if you knew that you were one with the pure creative energy of God and that you were shaping that energy all the time with your thoughts? If you knew this you could begin to connect the dots right now and see how your past thoughts, beliefs and feelings became alive, became your life. You would see that your story, which began as an invisible thought, started to grow arms and legs when you attached feelings to it. It walked everywhere with you and attracted the people and the experiences that made sense in the context of the story you had created. If you could grasp that you are the author of your stories, you would see that things had not happened to you but were happening through you.

One evening I was discussing with my students how the family sayings and stories that were handed down to us may actually be interfering with the life we are trying to create for ourselves. If we have adopted those sayings and stories as our own, they become part of the dots that will be out-pictured in our lives. When I said this, one of my students had a sudden realization. She had adopted her family's story.

Maria shared that she came from a long line of survivors dating back to the 1700s. The stories of the various concentration camps and overwhelming struggles of her ancestors were passed down from generation to generation. From an early age, she was taught that to be a survivor was something to be proud of, and she internalized that story. That was what she had placed upon the light, the creative energy of God, and that is exactly what her life looked like. She was a survivor all right. One horrendous, unfair and scary experience after another happened to her, and yet she survived. She survived things that you and I would never imagine could happen to one person in a lifetime.

That evening she woke up in the middle of the night and wrote page after page of all the things that she had survived. She couldn't believe how long it took to write it all down. She said it just kept coming. Once she got the story out of her, she looked at it, connected the dots between her beliefs about herself and her experiences, and decided right then that she was done with surviving. Instead, she was ready to see herself as thriving. The next time that we met for class you could visibly see the difference in her.

The next chapter will provide you with questions that will help you to discover your dots, the dots regarding the thoughts, feelings and beliefs that were in place during significant times in your life. They are what have created your experiences. The "dots" of your past are always involved in your everyday experiences. They will continue to affect your life in the same way until you change your story. By examining significant past relationships and/or challenging times involving money, health, career, family, etc., you can return to those moments in your mind and begin to make sense of your story. What *were* you thinking, believing and feeling about yourself and the world at that time? What story had you told yourself? What story were you living in?

Please understand that the same system of connecting the dots applies to your positive experiences too. It is just as important to connect the dots between your thoughts, feelings, beliefs and the experiences that you think of as the "good times" as it is to connect them to those you think of as the "bad times." Reflecting on the past, you will remember the people in your life. During the good times did you feel that you were around people who loved, supported and accepted you for who you were? Individuals in our lives are always a reflection of how we feel about ourselves.

We all have a tendency to rate our experiences, but the truth is that the creation process is the same for both positive and negative experiences. They are all shaped by the same creative energy of God that is always flowing through you.

Making sense of your past experiences translates into better understanding of your current experiences. You will begin to discover the answers to questions like, "Why me?" or "Why did I attract that person or that relationship or that situation?" You will also begin to discover the major themes in your life, and the "Why does this keep happening to me?" questions will begin to reveal their answers. You will discover that all of your relationships and experiences are mirrors reflecting your story and feelings about yourself and the world you live in. Because you have the gift of freewill, God, pure creative energy, allows you to be the author of your own creations. You discover that your experiences are all God-energy being shaped by your thoughts, feelings and beliefs. In this process of connecting the dots you will discover God in the midst of all of your experiences.

God has always been expressing through you and creating your experiences from whatever you chose to focus on. Connecting the dots of your thoughts, feelings and beliefs to your past experiences wakes you up to what is and always has been going on. Discovering that you have been creating experiences, exposes the creative energy (God) that has always been operating through you, and is moving in tandem with you.

You and God moving as one.
You and God as one.
You...God.

From this vantage point you will also begin to see that you have always been guided and encouraged by the discomfort of your challenging experiences to choose something better for yourself. Making the connection, as Maria did, transforms your old stories of something happening *to* you, to something happening *through* you. It turns your stories of victimhood into the sacred journey of your powerful soul. Your soul is a unique individual expression of God desiring to express fully through you. From this perspective, you begin to identify your own spiritual evolution. You begin to see that you have always been encouraged by your Higher Self, your inner God-self, to release the old stories that are not serving you and recognize your true identity and potential.

In the next chapter, you will begin the journey into your own story. If you are willing, you will find yourself moving from "Whys" to "Wise." You will begin to see your life with new eyes.

It is important to allow yourself to go as far back as you can to examine your hopes, your fears, your dreams and your beliefs because whatever you have set in motion stays in motion until you edit your story.

So, if for example, you grew up believing that money is the root of all evil, that thought will affect your experiences until you unearth that belief, question it and change it. Struggling to acquire money in the physical world will not change your financial status until you change your mind about money.

"If you do not change direction,
you may end up where you are going."
— Lao Tzu
604 BC– 531 BC

You are one with the pure creative energy of God, and that energy is always expressing through the stories that are held in your conscious and subconscious mind. Whether you realize it or not, you are always working with that pure creative energy. It is only when you recognize that you can choose your thoughts and their corresponding feelings that you begin to consciously create. In the meantime, you unconsciously create and attract persons and situations into your life that reflect your thoughts, feelings and beliefs. But everything and everyone is on purpose, and these "others," without realizing it, are part of your awakening. The discomfort you have felt with many of them served to move you forward on your path to self-acceptance and self-love. They got you this far, didn't they?

Don't worry, you don't have to remember everything. Once you get the hang of this, you will be able to follow the dots and make a connection as to why this or that happened or is happening. Using your own unique map of self-discovery, you can begin to consciously navigate the journey of your life in alignment with your authentic self, your soul.

It is the willingness to connect the dots and discover your truth that says to your subconscious mind that it is okay to reveal what has been hidden from you. As you connect the dots, your subconscious mind begins the work of rewiring your brain and building a new story. Old beliefs, thoughts and feelings of victimhood will begin to dissolve and be supplanted by new empowering beliefs, thoughts and feelings. When this happens, old painful patterns are broken, and your life begins anew.

———————

"Yesterday is gone and its tale told.
Today new seeds are growing."
— *Rumi*
September 30, 1207 – December 17, 1273

———————

So, now it is time to look backwards, to look at your beginning, your set-up in this life. Events that appeared to have happened in a haphazard way will begin to change their shape, and you will start to see with new eyes that it was all on purpose. It is time to look at your story.

Some things to remember on your journey:

- Thoughts are things; they are the transparencies that you have placed upon God, pure creative energy.

- Thoughts that evoke powerful emotions are then projected into your life by the creative energy, God.

- Thoughts without the emotional charge of feelings have no real power to manifest outcomes.

- Everything "out there" is really a reflection of what you think, feel and believe within.

- Your soul is powerful, knows where it wants to go and is coaxing you along.

- Any discomfort or upset you feel is on purpose and is an attempt to awaken you.

- Reviewing your past in a new way is key to recognizing God, pure creative energy, in the midst of your life.

- Your past holds the key to the discovery of your true identity and purpose.

- Be very gentle, kind, patient, loving and compassionate with yourself as you go through this process.

* * * * * * *

———————————

*"Everything that is in the heavens, on earth,
and under the earth is penetrated with connectedness,
penetrated with relatedness."*
— Hildegard of Bingen
September 16, 1098 – September 17, 1179

———————————

Chapter 6
The Set-Up

"Life can only be understood backwards;
but it must be lived forwards."
— Søren Kierkegaard
May 5, 1813 – November 11, 1855

Every story has a main character and a "set-up" complete with supporting characters, a purpose or theme, and conflicts and resolutions built within it. Let us begin with your story. You are the main character in your own story. In order to understand why you think and feel the way you do, and more importantly, why you have had your particular experiences, it is important to look at your history and your background. This is your set-up. This may at first appear to be merely a psychological mining for information, but you will find in a very short time that this excavating is not only about your psychology but also your spirituality. A very important part of your story got buried. That keeps you from realizing that your past and present life are not only about what happened *to* you, but also what has happened and is happening *through* you. The willingness to dig into your set-up will allow what has been hidden from your conscious mind to reveal itself. It will explain what has been creating your past and present experiences. It is about connecting the dots.

Find a quiet place to answer the questions on the following worksheets. Put down the first thing that comes to mind. Put aside any

71

thoughts of how you "should" answer these questions. These worksheets are for your eyes only. Being completely honest with yourself is the only path to true understanding. You are on a search for God already present in your life. This God is pure creative energy, a God that has been and still is creating *through* you. This creative energy, God, has been using your conscious and subconscious thoughts, feelings and beliefs to create your experiences. By answering the following questions, you will begin the process of exposing the stories that have been causing your experiences. Feel free to use separate paper to record your answers.

———————

"Be patient toward all that is unresolved in your heart
and try to love the questions themselves
like locked rooms and like books that are
written in a foreign tongue."
— Rainer Maria Rilke
December 4, 1875 – December 29, 1926

———————

EXPLORING YOUR SET-UP

1. What did you like to do as a child?

2. Were you allowed to choose what you would like to do with your time, or were the activities chosen for you?

3. Were you given the opportunity to explore different activities and artistic endeavors?

4. What activities did you enjoy doing alone?

5. What was your favorite thing to do with others?

6. Describe your "play time."

7. What did you like to wear?

8. Did you get to choose what you would wear? Explain.

9. What did you want to be when you grew up?

10. Did you do it or something related to it? Why? Why not?

11. Did you paint, sing, dance, build things, write, act, etc.? Make a list.

12. What activities did you feel you were especially good at? What made you think that?

13. Did you wet the bed? If so, how did your parent(s) respond?

14. Did you have any difficulties with your speech? If so, how did your parent(s) respond?

15. Did you find reading comprehension to be a challenge? If so, how did your parents respond?

16. Did you find school especially challenging? Why? How did your parents respond?

17. What did you feel were your greatest weaknesses, challenges? How did you come to that conclusion?

18. Were you active? Why or Why Not?

19. What physical activities did you enjoy? Were you given time for them? Why or why not?

20. What did you want to explore when you were young but were unable to pursue? Explain.

21. Describe your most embarrassing moment(s) as a child. Who was there? How did you feel?

22. How did you feel about the world you lived in? Why did you feel this way?

23. Describe your parents' relationship.

24. What role did your mother have in the family? Was she happy? Explain.

25. What role did your father have in the family? Was he happy? Explain.

26. Which parent did you feel most comfortable being around? Why?

27. Did you feel comfortable having others over to your house? Why?

28. The feelings that best describe how it felt to be at home with everyone are . . .

29. I was _____ in the birth order of my siblings.

30. I always felt that _____ was the favorite, and that made me feel...

31. I was treated like I was the _____ one in my family, and that made me feel... (Smart, lazy, creative, bad, cute, ugly, immature, responsible, etc.)

32. Do you still feel that way around your family?

33. The thing that I was most ashamed of when I was young was...

34. The thing I was most proud of when I was young was . . .

35. The thing that I felt guiltiest about was . . .

36. The most hurtful things said to me were . . .

37. What chores were you asked to do as a child?

38. Did you feel safe? Why or why not?

39. If I could have changed anything about my relationship with my mother back then, it would be . . .

40. If I could have changed anything about my relationship with my father back then, it would be . . .

41. Describe the God that you were taught about as a child.

42. My family felt that people who had a lot of money were . . .

43. My family felt that people who were poor were . . .

44. My parent(s) felt that people who drank were . . .

45. My parent(s) felt that people who were sick or unhealthy were . . .

46. My parent(s) felt that people who were overweight were . . .

47. My parent(s) felt that people who were thin were . . .

48. If someone got divorced, they were considered . . .

49. My parent(s) felt that people who were loud were . . .

50. My parent(s) felt that people who were successful were...

51. Did you have the feeling that there were things going on in your family that you didn't know about?

52. Did you feel that you could ask about those things? Why?

53. Were you allowed to show all of your emotions?

54. What happened if you expressed some of your feelings?

55. Did you feel that you were heard? In what way?

56. Did you feel respected? Can you give examples?

57. Did you feel you were treated fairly by your family? Your teachers? The world? Why or why not?

58. Were you afraid that one of your parents might leave?

59. Did you know why they would have left?

60. Did one or both of your parents leave? If so, what happened?

61. Did you feel valued as a child? Explain.

62. Your biggest fear as a child was . . .

63. Did your biggest fear come true? If so, describe it from the perspective of your child-self.

64. When I was growing up women were considered . . .

65. When I was growing up men were considered . . .

66. My parent(s) felt that gay men were . . .

67. My parent(s) felt that gay women were . . .

68. My parent(s) felt people of a different race/culture were . . .

69. This was especially true of . . .

70. I was taught that people of a different faith were . . .
This was especially true of . . .

71. Can you remember any family or religious sayings that might be standing in your way? If so, please list below. For example:
"Money is at the root of all evil."
"Life is hard."
"If you want something, you have to make it happen!"
"Don't get your hopes up, you'll only be disappointed."
"God never gives us more than we can handle."
"Trust no one."
"Never give up! Persevere!"
"We (last name) _____ come from a long line of _____." (alcoholics, survivors, health issues, etc.)

72. Do you remember receiving any criticisms from your family? If so, please list below.
e.g. "You'll never amount to anything."
"You're _____ (clumsy, stupid, fat, too tall, slow, ugly, lazy)."
"Who do you think you are?"

73. It is very likely that other memories came up for you that were not in this inventory. Please describe what they were and how they made you feel at that time?

74. Also, pay attention to your body and see if there is still discomfort, especially around your heart and stomach, when you examine certain memories. These are your Hot Spots.

* * * * * * * *

Chapter 7
Checking for Hotspots

"Your pain is the breaking of the shell
that encloses your understanding."
— Kahlil Gibran
January 6, 1883 – April 10, 1931

Remember the childhood game "Hot and Cold?" We used to love hiding things from one another and then guiding the seekers to find the hidden object by telling them when they were hot (very near the object) or cold (far away from the object). When they didn't know which way to go, we would say "warmer, warmer," or "cold, very cold," and they would correct their course. Sometimes, even when the object was in plain view, they couldn't see it because it blended in so easily with the background.

That is what we are going to do with the inventory that you created in the previous chapter. I want you to review your answers and find the hot spots. Any topics that brought up uncomfortable feelings are your hotspots. You may think that you have already addressed and "healed" these spots, but just as in the childhood game, they simply may have blended into your background, your subconscious mind. The subconscious mind, unlike your conscious mind, is operating 24/7 and it is influencing the blueprint that builds your present and future experiences. All of the thoughts, feelings and beliefs held in your conscious and subconscious mind are acted upon by the subjective, creative mind (God). So, if you think you have done your spiritual work, but still don't care for some of the experiences that are showing up in your life, it is time to see what was drafted a long time ago and make conscious revisions. Until you do that, God, creative energy, will continue to create your life based on the thoughts, feelings and beliefs you have within your conscious and subconscious mind.

So, do not be disappointed if you find some hotspots. Warm spots and hotspots are good! They are the inner promptings of your soul coaxing you to move from victimhood to empowerment. They are the buried treasures that you actually want to discover. They may not seem like treasures to you now, but excavating old hurts, fears and pain are necessary if you want to connect *all* of the dots and understand what has been running in the background and affecting the quality of your life.

You see, thoughts are transparent things, but feelings give them tremendous power. That is why empty affirmations, the ones that you say but do not really *feel*, have little power to change your experiences. Buried beliefs and feelings can wreak havoc on the most well-intentioned conscious thoughts.

For example, if you find yourself depleted and resenting others because you have no time or money for yourself, you need to look at what you've been taught about helping others. If you grew up in a codependent family or a religion that praised martyrs, saying "No" may be very hard for you. If you desire a joyful, balanced life for yourself but what is running in your subconscious mind is a belief that God wants you to say "Yes" even when you would like to say "No," it is going to be impossible for you to build that life until you think it through and make a revision.

Imagine what would happen if you had an architect designing a custom home for you based on your wants, desires and needs, but without your knowledge, others in your life were allowed to draw their own concepts of design onto your blueprint. Now, imagine if you refused to look at the final blueprint before it went into construction. You would not recognize the finished product. You would likely be asking to see the blueprint to discover why it didn't look like the home that you thought you were designing. That is what you're doing here; reviewing the whole blueprint for design flaws. Examining your set-up allows you to discover thoughts, feelings and beliefs placed there by others that don't match the life you've been trying to build for yourself. Your "blueprint" may include someone else's walls and views of the world. It may even include some old walls that you built yourself, perhaps necessary at the time they were constructed, but are now standing in the way of your good.

Now imagine that you want the architect to correct the construction and rebuild the home based on *your* design concepts alone, but you still refuse to look at the old blueprint and make the necessary revisions. Instead you tell the architect what you do want (affirmations) and feel as if you have taken a step in the right direction. Going forward, you expect to see signs of your desired improvements, but if what you want to build is incompatible with what has already been specified, the pre-existing blueprint without revision will influence all future construction. Every time the architect meets with the contractor to build from the plans, all they see is what was drawn there, even if *you* don't want to acknowledge it. Your architect and the contractor cannot build two things to occupy the same space. Only you can choose to look at what is there, order the demolition of the old walls (old thoughts and old beliefs), and make the revisions.

That is what is going on in the subconscious mind. Many of us are finding things in our lives that we don't want. We try to build our ideal life but keep bumping up against old walls that are preventing it from fully manifesting. This continues until we make conscious revisions.

You are about to find out what walls, in the form of thoughts, feelings and beliefs, are in place that have been preventing your best life.

You are about to shed light on what is written on your blueprint and stored in your subconscious mind. Those things, that you have resisted looking at, have been persisting in your life.

The next chapter will delve deeper into how the very thing we don't want to deal with will always show up in our life in some manner. You will soon discover why this dynamic exists. But beyond that, just know that it takes a tremendous amount of energy, energy that you are not even aware of expending, *not* to allow yourself to think of something that carries a lot of emotional charge. When you suppress your thoughts and feelings about unresolved issues, you depress yourself. Our addictions to food, sex, substances, drama, etc., can all be linked to a desire to "numb out" in order to block out uncomfortable feelings.

Do not worry, you will not be bringing these things up to mull them over. Instead, you will be bringing them up in order to neutralize them with a new perspective. When you do this, you will be surprised at how quickly they will lose their emotional charge. You will be amazed at how quickly blocked energy is released when you step into a new understanding. That energy will come pouring back into your body and into your life.

I've had individuals who have taken this course who initially refused to answer the questions in the previous chapter. They said it was too painful to step back into their childhood and remember what happened and how they felt. By the middle of the class, when they were provided with a new perspective, they felt free of the burden of carrying around the past, free to feel their feelings, free to live, free to love. Dropping years of emotional baggage is very liberating.

Look over your inventory from Chapter 6. Check for areas of emotional charge, like events, experiences and people, that you don't like to think about anymore. Know that what you resist will persist. It will persist as similar people and experiences showing up in your life. Remember the feeling of "Why does this keep happening to me?"

Resistance is a powerful magnet of what you don't want. So, lean into the following exercise and write down what you have been avoiding, thinking and feeling on a conscious level. Bring it into the light so that it can be healed and neutralized with a new perspective.

———————————

"The wound is the place
where the light enters you."
— Rumi
September 30, 1207 – December 17, 1273

———————————

Hotspots

This section is for listing the "Hotspots" that emerged while answering the questions in the previous chapter. Write a brief description of the people involved and the experiences. Don't worry about the number of hotspots cited. You may have one or two, you may have ten or more.

1.

2.

3.

4.

5.

6.

7.

8.

9.

10.

11.

12.

13.

14.

15.

* * * * * * *

Chapter 8
Stepping into Your Story

"Don't be satisfied with stories, how things have gone with others.
Unfold your own myth."
— Rumi
September 30, 1207 – December 17, 1273

Every story that we read, every movie that we watch, is created for its audiences' understanding. As we addressed in Chapter 6, there is always a set-up. During the set-up we are introduced to the lead character, the supporting players, how they came together and an idea of how they relate to one another. This set-up is fleshed out with the unique qualities of each character's personality based upon a not-so-obvious personal history. But as we observe them in the storyline, we feel that we come to know them and what to expect from them. Because of the set-up, the background given to us by the writers, we begin to gain insight as to why the main character thinks and behaves as they do.

Every good story is also filled with conflicts and challenges that test the integrity of the lead character. The author always provides at least one major challenge and theme for the lead. This is what makes the story interesting. We want to see how it will turn out, how they will handle the obstacles, overcome them and move forward as a better person.

What we don't like is a story with an obstacle and no resolution. We don't like it in our books, or our movies, and we certainly don't like it in our own lives. We all have had friends and acquaintances that have

91

been stuck. They've called us to lament. They've asked for advice. They've talked to everyone about it, but nothing seems to change. Perhaps you have felt that way at times. Perhaps you have stood so close to the picture that you could not see what the audience viewing the story of your life might clearly see. Occasionally, it is good to step back and take an inventory of our lives and gain the perspective of an observer.

Imagine that a movie is being produced to cover your journey through this world. Answer the following questions so that the writer, casting director and film director have some sense of who you felt you were throughout your teens, so that they can accurately portray you and your life.

1. Write a description of yourself beginning around age 13 and throughout your teens. Not how others saw you, but how you *felt* about yourself and your life so far. For examples, class clown, top of your game, outcast, different, attractive, ugly, average, athletic, artistic, poor, smart, etc.

2. How do you think others, like your peers, teachers, parents, siblings, etc., would describe you?

3. What did you think you wanted to do with your life?

4. Did you feel in control of your life? Explain.

5. How did you *feel* during your teens? (Circle any that apply or write in your own.)

Happy	Sad	Safe	Fearful	Smart
Stupid	Confident	Shy	Talented	Plain
Worthy	Unworthy	Secure	Insecure	Loved
Neglected	Alone	Unlovable	Creative	Empty
Normal	Different	Ashamed	Proud	Expendable
Cherished	Unique	Lost	Lazy	Alien

6. Which of these identities best describes how you would define yourself as a teen?

Victim	Survivor	Gifted One
Abuser	Damaged	One most likely to…?
Rescuer	Persevering	Guilty
Empowered One	Sinner	_____

(Fill in your own identity)

7. Why did you feel this way?

8. How did *you* feel about God and your relationship to/with God?

9. Did you say prayers that were given to you by others? Or did you speak or pray to God from your heart during challenging times? If so try to remember how you addressed God during this period of your life. Write an example of a prayer you said, or past conversation you had, during this time with God.

10. How did you feel about this thing called Life?

11. How did you feel about the world in which you lived?

* * * * * * *

Chapter 9
Casting Calls

Based on your answers about your adolescence from the previous chapter, describe the appearance, demeanor and experiences of the main character (you) in your "movie" in a way that would make sense to a viewing audience. How do you look? How do you act with people? How do you feel? Now, who would the supporting actors be? Who is the bad guy? Who is the best friend? Who is the love interest? You will probably find that all of your relationships and all of your experiences made sense for who you thought and felt you were at that time.

You will also find that as you moved through your life and made adjustments to your perception of yourself, that your appearance, demeanor, relationships and experiences changed to match that new perception. A person who has really low self-esteem because of their set-up (childhood) is probably not going to have an adolescence filled with great relationships and experiences, but instead a life that reflects someone that doesn't feel so good about themselves.

Look at all the movies going on around you. You will find that all the right actors are in place for everyone. If you have ever wondered why a talented friend is having a hard time making it in their particular field, or why their relationships are always derailing, or why they seem to be settling, look more closely. Listen to what they are saying and feeling about themselves and their world. You may see the answers. There is always a perfect reflection in the outer that matches the inner and outer dialogue of each individual. That is because the Law of Identity is always at work. Who you think, feel and believe yourself to be is always out-pictured as your life. When your friend changes their mind about themselves and the world they live in, their life will change. When you change your mind, your life will change. God is always asking you, "Who do *you* think you are?" and Its creative energy is responding to your innermost answer. Your relationships and experiences reflect your current identity.

Mirror, mirror, on the wall... Your relationships reflect your old and new identities.

If you are thinking that you couldn't possibly remember how you felt about yourself when you were first stepping out on your own, try looking at your past relationships and experiences for clues. The people in your life were always reflecting back to you who you believed yourself to be. They also mirrored how much love and acceptance you felt for yourself at the time.

Imagine yourself as an observer watching a show about your early adult life called, "This *Was* My Life."

1. Describe your first significant relationship.

2. Do you remember why you were you drawn to them? For example, they were so artistic, passionate, calm or excitable, distant or warm, a bad boy, the perfect lady, the life of the party, etc.

3. How did it turn out?

4. Did it match some old pattern from your family life? Did it remind you of how you felt with one of your parents? If so, in what way?

5. How did you *feel* in your first significant relationship? Respected? Loved? Inadequate? Abused? Nurtured? Special? Unworthy? Important?

6. Describe your next significant relationship.

7. How did you feel?

8. Did you learn something new about yourself in each relationship?

9. Describe a turning point in your life.

10. Did you take it? Why or why not?

11. Did you send anyone away that actually would have been good for you in order to be with someone that was not so good for you?

12. Do you remember why you made that choice?

13. List the names of significant friends that you've had over the years.

14. How did you feel in each significant friendship?

15. Are you still friends? Look at each one and ask yourself why or why not?

16. Did they make sense for who you thought you were at the time?

17. Did any of them stop making sense? What did you do about it?

18. How do your current friends compare with friends from the past? Are they a better match for who you are now? Did your earlier friendships match who you felt yourself to be at that time?

19. How did you feel in your various relationships and friendships? Loved? Supported? Nourished? Criticized? Respected? Dismissed?

20. Looking over your friendships, would you say that they behaved as friends, like one of your parents or like "frenemies"—enemies disguised as friends?

21. If they were similar to a parent, which one? Explain.

22. If they seemed more like an enemy, describe their jabs or less-than-loving behavior?

What you did for a living
also provides clues of your past identities.

1. List your various jobs.

2. How did your bosses treat you?

3. How did your co-workers treat you?

4. Were you ever fired? Why?

5. Did you ever resign? Why?

6. How did you feel in your jobs? Supported? Respected? Criticized? Encouraged?

7. Review your work history. Were there some work relationships that mirrored your family relationships? Did a boss or co-worker remind you of a parent?

8. If so, which one? How did they make you feel about yourself?

Now imagine yourself as an observer watching a show about your current life called, "This *Is* My Life" Who do you think and feel you are today?

1. Describe your life now.
   Work:

   Intimate Relationship:

   Friends:

   Home:

   Auto:

   Health:

   Mood:

   Finances:

2. As you changed, did the people and experiences in your life change? Explain.

3. Did they get better or worse? Explain.

4. If you feel your life improved, who or what most helped you to get to where you are today? There may be several examples and individuals. Really think about the answer.

Surprisingly, being fed up with a person or situation is the best catalyst for growth and change. It gets you to the place of not necessarily knowing what you will do next but knowing you won't be doing *that* any longer. Who or what was your perfect "last straw" that made you finally put an end to *being* one way in the world and open to another? Who or what made you choose a better life for yourself?

Look at your answer to number 4. "Who or what most helped you to get where you are today?" Make sure you give them special recognition when you roll the credits of your story, for without them you would not be where you are today. You see, even what you thought was wrong, turned out to be right. All was not as it seemed. You are getting fitted with new eyes. You are beginning to connect the dots and see that everything and everyone was and is on purpose. There are no accidents or chance encounters. You are beginning to see that as you adjusted your thoughts, beliefs and feelings about yourself, your experiences changed.

Now ponder why those particular people and experiences came to be on your path. Is it possible that you have been guided and encouraged to love yourself and move into the truth of who you are? Is it conceivable that you live in a mutually supportive universe and that the truth of your creative power and purpose are being revealed to you? Could it be that God is speaking into your life and has always been speaking to you through your experiences?

Consider that all of your experiences have been invitations addressed to you to look deeper and discover the creative power of God living within you. What you've been searching for was merely hidden beneath all the stories given to you by others. God was always there in the midst of your life. You and God are intimately connected, inseparable, one.

* * * * * * *

Chapter 10
Dismantling Your Story

"The greatest discovery of my generation is that
a human being can alter his life by
altering his attitudes of mind."
— William James
January 11, 1842 – August 26, 1910

So, we've spent some time looking over your life. I promised you that we were not reviewing it to ruminate in the past. This book is about reviewing your life to find if God has always been present in your experiences. You may think that God was absent or neglectful. Perhaps that was your experience with your physical parents. God was not absent. God was incredibly present, more present than anybody has ever been to you. The problem is that, like most people, you imagined God as a personality existing outside of yourself. Perhaps you saw God as a deity that would hand out rewards or punishments, smiling on some and turning his back on others. Yes, most people also imagine God as male. Those visual images, depicted throughout centuries, of a man with a long white beard and flowing robes looking down upon us may be hard to delete, but removing those images from your mind is a game changer.

One of the greatest revisions you will ever make to your story is your definition of God. Instead of seeing God as a personality, imagine God, not with a body, but as pure creative energy, not seen but unseen, not judging but allowing, like electricity. Electricity will bring to life whatever you choose to plug into it. Likewise, God, pure creative energy, brings to life the thoughts, feelings and beliefs that you are plugged into. You and God have always moved everywhere as a unit, with you as the thinker of thoughts and God as the creative energy acting upon your thoughts. God expresses as everything that your personality feels and believes.

Your thoughts, feelings and beliefs are constantly changing, so they are not God, but are instead what God, creative energy, acts upon. And this is what this book is about; your personality becoming aware of God, aware of a powerful creative energy that is underpinning all of your experiences. God is the creative energy that acts upon your personality's stories.

If you can truly entertain this new description of an intimate God, you will find that it cannot exist concurrently with your old concept of a deity that exists beyond your reach. If you can ponder this new definition of God, you will be well on your way to revising your own story. In an instant, your perspective can change. You will begin to see that you've come into this life for a purpose, and your early stories were just your set-up. If you look at all of the positive changes in the world, you can see that many people born into a variety of challenging family backgrounds overcame them by revising their stories. They realized that their early experiences were on purpose and necessary to create new thoughts, feelings and beliefs. Their revisions created opportunities to break old cycles, remove stigmas and heal the shame that plagues so many. Their revisions allowed them to love themselves and others. That is what is here for you.

Your early set-up is the personal experience that allows you to discover and speak from your authentic voice, the voice of your Higher Self, a voice that will change perceptions and heal our world. Whatever your early experiences, your purpose is woven into them. Many people do not realize this, and they get caught in their set-up and build an entire life reliving and reacting to what happened to them. Unknowingly they are creating similar experiences for themselves because they are focused on the past. The truth is that nothing happened to you. It happened through you. It always has, and it always will.

What we are going to work on next in this chapter is very powerful. In any story, the narrative can be told from the perspective of different characters. It is the author's prerogative to decide who will tell the story. For most of us, we allowed our personality, our lower self, to tell the story. We believed that we could be harmed. We believed that we were victims of another. The same story told from the perspective of your authentic self, your Higher Self, reads quite differently. It is like night and day. Let's compare the stories from the two perspectives.

Your lower self believes in physical lineage. It believes that your lineage creates your family tree and that you are a direct product of your mother and father. They are a product of their mother and father and so on and so on. Your siblings, aunts, uncles and children fill up the branches of this purely physical tree.

This tree then produces fruit (people and lives) that are imprinted with all manner of inheritances like depression, disease, health, intelligence, talents or lack of talents. What is possible is based on world beliefs and what has been accomplished hitherto by others. Fears and belief in lack are passed down from generation to generation. The goal of this approach to life is to try to get through it as best you can and hope there is a reward at the end of this life when the body dies.

Your Higher Self knows that all of the beliefs of the lower self simply act as filters that God, creative energy, projects through. It knows that if you change the filter, the belief, the projection changes. It knows that this life is an out-picturing of the thoughts, beliefs and feelings of the individual. It knows there is no real thing called limitation or disease. There is no such thing as an inheritance of lack, mental abilities or talents from another physical being. Our lineage leads beyond the physical to our true source, God. So, whatever God is, that is what is truly inherited. The desire to express in a certain manner and exhibit certain talents and abilities are evidence of the unique seeds of God that were planted in the individual. Your Higher Self knows that it chose to come here and that it has work to do. The work is to remove the filters of the lower self from the world and allow the pure creative energy of God to shine through. Look at the examples on the following pages. See if you can identify the story you've been living in the majority of the time.

Examples of Lower Self's Story—The Victim
"Things just happen *to me.*"

"I just got dealt a bad start with bad parents."

"I am damaged goods and my past defines me."

"I know that God doesn't give me more than I can handle, and I should learn to handle it."

"I am at risk to inherit family diseases and mental health issues."

"My family is prone to addictions of alcohol, drugs, etc."

"I am susceptible and must be on the look-out for all new diseases."

"I am not worthy."

"It is hard to find a good partner and have a healthy relationship."

"Life is tough, and you have to work hard to have a quality life."

"Death is terrible and something to be feared."

"There are only so many possibilities."

"War and poverty are inevitable."

"There is only so much _____ to go around."

"We all inherited Original Sin."

"There will be a Judgment Day."

"Heaven and Hell are real places."

I know that this sounds rather glum, but if you turn on the news or walk into many churches, you will find that these lower-self stories are their main focus. From this perspective your experiences are outside of your control. According to the lower-self's story you are a sitting duck in danger of inheriting your family's physical and mental maladies. Your feelings and behaviors, like anger, rage, emotional availability, coping skills, etc., are the result of what "they" did to you and there's not a lot you can do about it. In this story you are a victim of your parents, your childhood, the world, diseases, terrorism, the economy, the government and God. In this story, you see yourself as imperfect, and your early life as something that just happened to you. You may even hope that at the end of this lifetime you will be judged as being worthy of God's rewards.

Examples of Higher Self's Story—The Empowered One "Things happen *through me.*"

"I am a direct descendant of God."

"I am a unique and individual expression of God."

"God is my true parent, my true source, the source of everyone."

"I share the same parent, same source, with my "physical parents.""

"I know the ones I call "parents" are actually just fellow travelers."

"My original set-up in this life is key to my purpose."

Your True Inheritance

The power to create with thoughts, feelings and beliefs
The ability to focus attention and create from my desires
The ability to change directions, make adjustments
and affect the quality of my life
The ability to experience joy in the small things
The ability to diffuse challenges with Truth and
return to inner peace

Unlimited potential and possibilities
The ability to create a harmonious life
Access to abundance in all its forms—health, money,
relationships, beauty, etc.
Discovery of my purpose
The ability to create and live an authentic life
The ability to feel love and have compassion for myself and others
Healthy, loving and supportive relationships
Knowledge and reliance on the Universal Laws
Eternal life
Knowledge and experience of a direct connection with God
Unconditional love and support of God

---

*"What lies behind us and what lies before us
are tiny matters compared to what lies within us."*
— *Ralph Waldo Emerson*
May 25, 1803– April 27, 1882

So, what do you choose for yourself? Will you stay captive in the story of your past? Are you ready to remove your parents from the position of ongoing power that you've given them, place them gently beside you and say, "Hello, fellow traveler"? What story will you live in from this moment on? Do you need the pity of others and the excuse of why your life does not work because of your upbringing? Or do you desire to know who and what you really are, your true origin before you came into the physical plane and all that you have inherited because of that divine lineage?

---

*"You were born with wings,
why prefer to crawl through life."*
— *Rumi*
September 30, 1207 – December 17, 1273

So many people have been told that they are sinners and that they are not worthy. The word "sin" is actually an old archery term meaning to miss the mark. Could it be that your only sin has been to miss the mark? Everybody misses the mark in their lives. Consider that your original "sin," your original missing of the mark, was only because you had been misinformed about your true identity by others who were also misinformed of their true identity. As William James said in the opening quote of this chapter, it is never too late in life to alter your story.

Consider that your true story is that of one coming directly from God, as an individual expression of God, into the physical plane with the purpose to bring more love and light to this world. In order to accomplish your unique purpose, you needed the very experiences that you have had. These first-hand experiences allowed you to feel yourself a victim so that you could relate to others who feel that way. Your desire for an inner connection with your true Source, with God, moved you from victimhood to empowerment and allowed you to find your voice. You are one of many who are teaching others that it is okay to speak their truth and share their stories. This sharing of stories continually heals you and all who have had similar experiences. These healed individuals then have the courage to share their stories. Before long, people that felt they were victims of their early childhood experiences see that they are not alone and discover the purpose in those experiences. They are able to release the shame or guilt that they've held for so long and discover an inner strength that they never felt before. They are not damaged. They discover that they do not need to live small, but instead can become part of a movement bringing these experiences into the light where they can be healed and eradicated.

"There's a place in the soul
where you've never been wounded."
— Meister Eckhart
1260 – 1328 AD

When you share your unique story with those who need to hear it, you find yourself standing in the same place but living from a different state of mind. You have moved from the identity of Victim to Empowered One. You are one of those inhabiting this earth who are bringing more light and love into the world. Perhaps you are one of those, who in the process of dismantling your own victim story, have revealed yet another example of the pain caused by the hidden cycles of abuse, suicide, poverty and addiction. These cycles were allowed to thrive throughout history because of the silence and stigmas that surrounded them. As Carl Jung, modern psychologist said, evil in society is allowed to exist because people have been unable to tell their story. When you find your voice, you not only begin the process of healing yourself, you also play an important part in healing others, protecting others, and healing the world.

And this is the answer to "Why." This is the reason that you came into the world, into your particular family dynamic. This is why you had the parents and the experiences that you had. This is your purpose. This is God in your life. You were much braver before you came into this world, but you forgot who you were, and you became afraid. That bravery is accessible to you now.

So, you get to choose your story, that of the lower or Higher Self. In the first scenario, you try to live up to an outer God's expectations and hopefully meet your maker at the end of your physical life. In the second scenario God is as close as your breath, expressing through you and as you.

It is up to you to choose. You've spent a lot of time reviewing your life. You've seen how your ever-changing view of yourself changed your experiences. Is that not proof of God, as pure creative energy, projecting itself through your thoughts, feelings and beliefs? So, if the purpose of reading this book is to find the presence of God in your life, isn't the recognition of your evolving sense of self, past and present, and your corresponding experiences proof of that presence? What would happen if you took a deep breath and found God inside your breath, in every cell of your body, at the center of your thoughts, in your mind and in your heart and your heart's desires?

"Between God and Me
there is no 'Between'."
— Meister Eckhart
1260 AD – 1328 AD

---

* * * * * * *

Chapter 11
Search and Recovery

Now let's start searching for and connecting some dots between your past and current challenges to your thoughts, feelings and beliefs. Remember that viewing the world strictly from the personality's perspective, our lower self, the problem always appears to be "out there" caused by something or someone beyond its control—a victim of circumstances. It then begins to try to manage, manipulate and fix the outer problem in outer ways. In the process it focuses all of its attention on managing the "problem," which only makes matters worse. Focusing your attention on what you do not desire to experience is still focusing your attention on it. Remember the Laws of Attraction and Reciprocity? Without realizing it, that approach only serves to upset you and make the appearance of the "problem" more concrete and more abundant in your life.

When we switch to the perspective of our Higher Self, we know that we are always dealing with projections. We know that we only need to be completely honest and examine our true thoughts, feelings and beliefs to see how the situation was *really* created. We now know that if we change our perception about the situation, the projection will change. When we see the "problem" as a wake-up call guiding us to examine our thoughts and teaching us to take our minds off of what we *don't* want and put it on what we *do* want, it has served its purpose. The "problem" also reveals the existence of the Universal Laws that are simply, beautifully and impersonally working through our consciousness.

So, what is really going on is not a problem outside of us, but instead it is a result of erroneous thoughts, feelings and beliefs being projected by the creative energy of God within us. Any upset that we feel is simply our Higher Self trying to get our attention. Discomfort is a very effective way of doing that. God is simply extending Itself within your experiences, and the resulting discomfort serves to awaken you to the fact that you've forgotten your true identity and fallen into a victim mentality. By taking your attention off of what you don't want and choosing new thoughts, you acknowledge and use the creative power, God, within you. All that happened was that you had fallen asleep to your true nature and the nature of God, and began unconsciously creating. But now you are becoming awake and aware and you can use that awareness to consciously create what you desire.

———————

"You suppose that you are the lock on the door,
but you are the key that opens it. "
— Rumi
September 30, 1207 – December 17, 1273

———————

Look at the Sample Search and Recovery Worksheets in the following section. In these samples, there are six steps:

1. Identifying the Problem

2. Getting Honest with Yourself

3. Acknowledging the Power of Your Feelings

4. Seeing with New Eyes

5. Recognizing the Universal Law(s) at Work

6. Recovering Your True Identity

After the two sample worksheets, there are blank ones you can use for whatever challenge you choose to examine. It is important to be completely honest with yourself—no one is judging. This should be for your eyes only. You can say what is or what was really going on for you. Divulge the thoughts, feelings and beliefs that you might not admit to others. Without being honest you will not be able to connect the dots. You will not see how your true thoughts, feeling and beliefs are being acted upon by the creative energy, God.

Feel free to make copies of these worksheets. Eventually, you will not need the worksheets. You will be able to do all of this in your mind and see beyond what is going on in your life, good or bad, and identify your thoughts, feelings and beliefs that are creating a situation. If you have a perceived challenge before you, you will be able to see around it and recognize its true cause. You will be able to recognize the Universal Laws at work. You will know that the challenge is there so that you can let go of thoughts and beliefs that do not serve you. As you release these thoughts and beliefs, and replace them with empowering thoughts, you will find your life becoming easier and simpler. There will be less drama and more joy.

When you have changed your thoughts, you will have caused a new effect. By allowing yourself to focus on what you would love, you will begin attracting what you love. That love will go out into the world, benefit the world and return to you. You have learned to connect the dots and see everything on purpose. You have found God in your life. Use your life. Use your past to change and benefit the world. The world is waiting for you to be you.

.

Sample
Search and Recovery
Worksheets

SAMPLE #1 SEARCH AND RECOVERY
WORKSHEET—THE CHALLENGE

1. Identifying the Problem

Lower-Self's Story—Things just happen to me.

"It is so unfair! I was suddenly fired from my job!"

2. Getting Honest with Myself

What's really been going on in my life?

"I hated my job for a long time and always thought about how happy I would be when I could stop working there. My boss was emotionally abusive and the job unfulfilling. I would have resigned but I believed the job market was terrible, and I had bills. I was just afraid to leave."

3. Acknowledging the Power of My Feelings

"By showing up as this experience, God is revealing Itself to me as the loving creative energy that projects what I am thinking, feeling and believing.

If what I really desired was to leave this job, then it had to happen in some form. The real reason I was fired was because I really wanted to leave, but I was too afraid to resign. The creative energy of God always follows my true feelings."

4. Seeing with New Eyes

"I am ready to see this experience as a wake-up call and as loving guidance moving me along on my journey from victimhood to empowerment. I realize that I am being urged to let go of any limiting beliefs I hold regarding job opportunities. I am being asked to replace any thoughts of lack with a vision of my heart's desire. I trust that I can live my best life receiving all the good that is being offered to me."

5. Recognizing the Impersonal and Reliable Universal Law(s)

"If I choose, I can identify the Universal Law(s) at work. I can see the Laws of Attraction and Cause and Effect at work in this experience. If I want to attract something new into my life, I need to stop thinking about what I don't want and begin thinking about what I do want. I also need to replace any beliefs about a poor job market and open my mind to the unlimited possibilities available to me."

Identity   Attraction   Cause and Effect   Reciprocity

6. Recovering My True Identity
Higher-Self's Story—Things happen through me.

"I can see that this situation is merely a reflection and projection of my thoughts, feelings and beliefs. I always attract the perfect persons and situations to awaken me to my truth. In this moment I remember that I am one with God. Because God is my source and the source of all things, I acknowledge my true identity and begin to consciously create what I would love to see and feel in my life."

SAMPLE #2 SEARCH AND RECOVERY WORKSHEET—THE CHALLENGE

1. Identifying the Problem

Lower-Self's Story—Things just happen to me.

"I suddenly feel a lot of pain in the soles of my feet. It hurts so much that I'm afraid to stand up and move around. Why is this happening to me?"

2. Getting Honest with Myself

What's really been going on in my life?

"I really want to get out of my current relationship, but I am afraid because I believe that if I leave this relationship, I won't be able to make it on my own. I am afraid that I won't be able to stand on my own two feet. I really want to leave and feel I should, but I am afraid that I will be destitute. I have no real means of support."

3. Acknowledging the Power of My Feelings

"By showing up as this experience, God is revealing Itself to me as the loving creative energy that will always manifest what I am thinking, feeling and believing.

Because I hold a belief about not being able to support myself it hurts when I physically try to stand on my own two feet. I know that it is wrong to stay in something that is not right for me simply for security. Also, it is not fair to the other person involved. I know that my Higher Self is nudging me to remember that God is my only true source of abundance and support."

4. Seeing with New Eyes

"I am ready to see this physical discomfort as a wake-up call reminding me to recognize that my only true source of support is God. I am being urged to trust and rely on that support and to begin to live an authentic life."

5. Recognizing the Impersonal and Reliable Universal Law(s)

"If I choose, I can identify the Universal Law(s) at work."

"Identity, Attraction, and Cause and Effect"

Identity   Attraction   Cause and Effect   Reciprocity

6. Recovering My True Identity

Higher-Self's Story—Things happen through me.

"I can now see that this discomfort is a result of inaccurate thoughts, feelings and beliefs I hold about myself and the true source of all support. Even though this physical symptom is painful, so is living without spiritual integrity and staying in a relationship that does not reflect my authentic self. I know that I was urged to do this sooner, but I ignored the inner guidance I received. I tried to convince myself that I could stick with this relationship. I am grateful for this physical discomfort that is letting me know that playing a game on my God and my authentic self will never work. In this moment, I choose to begin to imagine a life I would love. I know that God is my source and I am one with God. I know that God planted the seeds of my desired life within me, and that I will be completely supported in living my authentic life."

SEARCH AND RECOVERY
WORKSHEET—PAST CHALLENGE

1. Identifying the Problem
Lower-Self's Story—Things just happen to me.

_____

_____

_____

2. Getting Honest with Myself
"If I am a spiritual being and God is my true parent and only source, then abundance in its many forms is my divine inheritance. If I was experiencing lack in any form, then my past challenge was about something other than what it appeared to be. This past situation served in awakening me to what I had been unconsciously creating through the thoughts, feelings and or beliefs that I had been holding about myself and/or my world. If I am completely honest with myself, I think this challenge was really about..."

_____

_____

_____

3. Acknowledging the Power of My Feelings
"By showing up in this part of my body or as this experience, my Higher Self, God, is revealing to me that I ..."

_____

_____

_____

124

4. Seeing with New Eyes

"I am ready to see this, to recognize the support of God urging me to live my truth, to live my best life, and to receive all the good that is being offered to me."

5. Recognizing the Impersonal and Reliable Universal Law(s)

"If I choose, I can identify the Universal Law(s) in action."

Identity   Attraction   Cause and Effect   Reciprocity

6. Recovering My True Identity

Higher-Self's Story—Things happen through me.

"I can now see that this situation was a reflection and projection of my thoughts, feelings and beliefs. I attracted the perfect person(s) and situation(s) to awaken me to my truth. I now see that this particular experience matched the vibration of feelings that I was carrying around in the world. I can see how I attracted it with my limiting beliefs about myself, God and the world I live in. In this moment, I remember who I am, an individual expression of God who desires that I live authentically, abundantly and joyfully. I now allow myself to embrace all the gifts inherent to my true identity."

SEARCH AND RECOVERY
WORKSHEET—CURRENT CHALLENGE

1. Identifying the Problem
Lower-Self's Story—Things just happen to me.

_____

_____

_____

2. Getting Honest with Myself
"If I am a spiritual being and God is my true parent and only source, then abundance in its many forms is my divine inheritance. If I am experiencing lack in any form, then my present challenge is about something other than what it appears to be. This present situation serves in awakening me to what I have been unconsciously creating through the thoughts, feelings or beliefs that I have been holding about myself and/or my world. If I am completely honest with myself, I think it is really about my belief that..."

_____

_____

_____

3. Acknowledging the Power of My Feelings
"By showing up in this part of my body, or as this experience, my Higher Self, God, is revealing to me that..."

_____

_____

_____

4. Seeing with New Eyes

"I am ready to see this, to recognize the support of God urging me to live my truth, to live my best life, and to receive all of the good that is being offered to me."

5. Recognizing the Impersonal and Reliable Universal Law(s)

"If I choose, I can identify the Universal Law(s) in action."

Identity   Attraction   Cause and Effect   Reciprocity

6. Recovering My True Identity

The Higher-Self's Story—Things happen through me.

"I can see that this situation is a reflection and projection of my thoughts, feelings and beliefs. I attracted the perfect person(s) and situation(s) to awaken me to my truth. I now see that this particular experience matches the vibration of feelings that I was carrying around in the world. I can see how I attracted it with my limiting beliefs about myself, God and the world I live in. In this moment, I remember who I am, an individual expression of God who desires that I live authentically, abundantly and joyfully. I now allow myself to embrace all the gifts inherent to my true identity."

Conclusion—Moving Forward

Letting go of the concept of a judgmental God is a vital first step in discovering the connection between ourselves and the loving creative energy that flows through us. When you stop seeing God as a personality, you can see that God is pure creative energy, and that this energy is the source of all. Everything is connected, but in order to see it for yourself you must slow down. You must read the subtext of what is and has been going on in your life. When you do, you will discover that every experience you have had, and every person you have met are all guiding you to your authentic self.

Remember that you are not alone on your journey. You have many teachers. You have an inner teacher that you can always turn to for guidance. You also have many outer teachers. In fact, all who come into your experience are teachers, but they are not teachers in the traditional sense. They do not wear robes and carry books. They are not teaching by speaking words and explaining ideas, but instead, they are teaching you through the examples of their lives, the stories they live in, and the effect they have on you.

Look at your life and see if you can identify your teachers. What they are offering you, without realizing it, is a look at how the Universal Laws work. By looking at their experiences and seeing what story they are living in, you can choose what story you want to live in and what you want to experience.

Choosing what you desire for yourself is not being judgmental of others. Instead, you can use discernment to see if the outcome they are experiencing is an outcome you desire. Judgment is looking out and deciding if something or someone is right or wrong, good or bad. Discernment is looking within and deciding if the experience you are observing is a good fit for you.

Judging is something our unenlightened personality does. As we emotionally and spiritually mature, we can begin to use discernment. We can observe people who are very judgmental and see how their need to be right, and to make others wrong, rules their lives. We can learn from them and choose something different for ourselves.

In this way, everything you experience is teaching you. Everything is supporting your unfoldment. The endings and beginnings of jobs or relationships, the ease or difficulty of projects, the discomfort and the healing of our bodies; these are all signposts. When we begin to connect the dots and see how everyone and everything is in place to move us toward living a more authentic life, we begin to see that we are living in what the New Thought writer, Arnold Patent, calls a mutual support system.

Even our disillusionment serves a purpose. When we become disillusioned with the world, many of us turn within. Later, we realize that our disillusionment was the doorway to a wisdom and a connection that cannot be contradicted or studied but simply felt and owned.

———————

"When you realize how perfect everything is
you will tilt your head back and laugh at the sky."
— Gautama Buddha
Approx. 563 BC – 483 BC

———————

When you connect the dots, you begin to see God intimately woven into every detail of your life. You begin to see your trials as invitations to see through the illusions of this world. You begin to see that your good has always been waiting for you just on the other side of your limiting thoughts, feelings and beliefs. No longer trapped by restricting thoughts, you can now move more easily through any challenges and into the presence of All That Is. You will begin to see synchronistic events and meaningful coincidences come into your life because *you* are opening the door to your infinite God-self.

Most of us have so many stories, so many thoughts and beliefs that actually prevent the experiences we desire from moving easily into our lives. Many of our thoughts are conflicting and that creates a reflection of chaos and turmoil. The solution? Clear the slate. Remove all the stories that you've placed over your authentic self and God and what will you find? You will find only the Light, that pure creative energy, God. Everything is God. But God is not a person or a personality. Therefore, your personality is not God. But the thoughts your personality has and has had, transform the pure creative energy into a projection of an experience in your world and the world at large.

People are always asking, "How could God allow this or that"? They ask as if God is a personality.

You would not ask an overhead projector why it is projecting exactly what you placed upon its lightbox. If you wrote the thoughts, the stories, that are written upon the transparencies that the Light projects through, you would not ask the projector why you wrote those thoughts. We should only be asking ourselves why we had those thoughts, and if we want to keep them.

But instead, we try to make the Light, the creative energy, God, responsible for our thoughts, our stories and all of our experiences. In effect, we are trying to hand back the freewill given to us. We are attempting to play small and deny the power of God within us. We are trying not to take any responsibility for what is being projected through our thoughts, feelings and beliefs. But that does not change the reality.

Here is a step by step summary of how to move forward. Now it is up to you.

Working with the Light, the Creative God-Energy

1. **First, contemplate what God is: Pure creative energy.** When you do this, you let go of God as a personality outside of you and acknowledge God as the Light, the creative energy within you projecting through you. Now, imagine yourself lifting your whole stack of accumulated thoughts and beliefs off the projector and seeing what is at the bottom of everything. It is pure God, pure creative unformed energy.

2. **Connect with God through your authentic self.** Pay attention to who or what drains you or energizes you. Your energy or lack of energy is your internal guidance system leading you to your authentic self, your God-Self. What energizes you connects you.

3. **Ask for guidance.** When a challenge arises, ask your inner teacher for guidance and then listen and pay close attention to what happens next in your life. Guidance comes in many forms, but it will come. Be ready to receive it. Just recognizing a steady stream of obstacles on your path as "No" and things easily falling into place as "Yes," is a great start. Hitting your head against the proverbial wall simply means, "Turn around and do something completely different."

4. **Always remain open to acquiring higher understanding.** Examine your thoughts and beliefs regarding any issues that are causing you concern. Look at them one by one and decide which ones you want to remain upon the Light, the pure creative energy, God, that is projecting through them. Look for conflicting or contradictory thoughts and beliefs. Make sure your thoughts and beliefs support your true divine identity.

5. **Make sure your authentic self is in the driver's seat.** Decide what you would love to do in this life and make it your priority, your focal point. Train your social self only to do the work of getting you there on time and dressed appropriately. When you do this, a whole stack of unnecessary "shoulds" are removed from the Light. The simpler you keep it, the more intensely and effortlessly the pure creative loving energy, God, can project through you.

6. **Make sure you are placing upon the Light what you want and *not* what you do not want.** It is very easy for people to fall into this habit because the world is often focusing on what we want to avoid. Instead of stating, "I don't want…" "I would hate it if…" "I'm afraid that…" "I can't stand…" say to yourself, "I would love…" "I can see myself…" Then fill in the picture and visualize it until you feel it.

7. **Take your hands off of the how.** When you do this, you are removing all the obstacles that your personality has attached to your desired outcome. When you take your hands off the "how," a whole stack of your world beliefs and social beliefs are removed from the Light, and fear is no longer written all over your transparencies, your thoughts.

8. **Then let it go. Feel the relief.** Your part is over. You've placed upon the Light, the pure creative energy, your heart's desires.

9. **Trust. Know that if it is yours, you will have it.** If not, it is not meant for you and something better will come along that will be a match for your authentic self, God expressing through you as you.

Your God, Your Thoughts, Your Life.

* * * * * * *

About the Author

Dana Winter, born in St. Louis, Missouri, to a critical mother and a loving but alcoholic father, grew up hiding her feelings of not being good enough by becoming a lifeguard, a cheerleader and a flight attendant. These attempts at creating a "happy" façade to mask her low self-esteem, led her to a series of confusing and abusive relationships until she finally chose to be authentic.

When she began searching for what she truly loved, things fell into place. Drawn to renovating homes and designing spaces, she got a degree in interior design, established her own design business, taught interior design and worked on large corporate special events. Most importantly, she began connecting the dots between living authentically and the abundant support available from the universe. Exploring and following her heart's desires led her to a new definition of God and the discovery that authenticity is the only path to true connection. God is creative energy expressing through us and as us.

One day she woke up and was through with design. A counselor suggested that since her spiritual connection was the most important thing to her that she consider becoming a minister or spiritual teacher. Two days later she was invited to speak at a Divine Science Church. There she discovered her true passion; to help others find their direct spiritual connection by living from their authentic selves.

She began her ministerial studies through the Brooks Center for Spirituality in Denver, Colorado, while serving as spiritual mentor of the church where she first spoke. She founded Harmony Fellowship in 2008 and continues to encourage others to live authentically through her Sunday talks, counseling, speaking engagements, and courses she created like *You…God, Connecting the Dots.*

CONTACT
For information about counseling, workshops or speaking
engagements email Dana Winter at danawinter@msn.com

Made in the USA
Columbia, SC
14 April 2024

34195320R00085